U.S. SPECIAL OPERATIONS

the forerunner spirit and the end time church

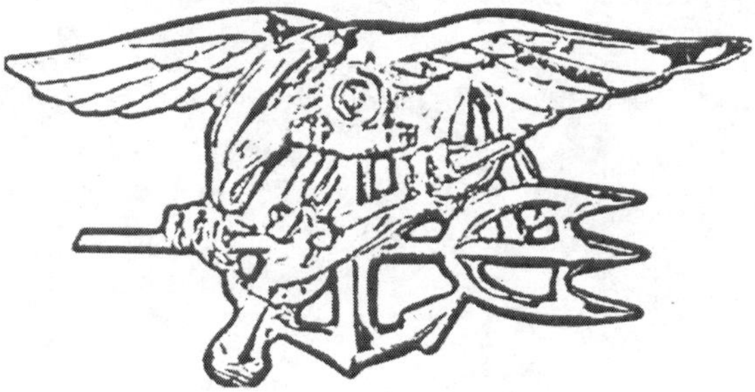

BEAU WALSH

Tate Publishing & *Enterprises*

“U.S. Special Operations: The Forerunner Sprit and the End Time Church”
by Beau Walsh

Published in the United States of America
by Tate Publishing, LLC
127 East Trade Center Terrace
Mustang, OK 73064
(888) 361–9473

ISBN: 1–5988642–5–4

060705

Table of Contents

Introduction

Throughout the years, I have found my life being guided or pushed along by the winds of change. One thing is for certain, my life will never stay the same for too long because I live in a transitional state of existence; I am always going from one event or place to another. I have been blessed with many opportunities in my life, and I am deeply grateful to the Lord for each and every one.

I was raised in a God-fearing home with parents who loved me. My father and mother have both served in the ministry for almost as long as I can remember. They gave their lives to the Lord when I was five years of age, and they have never looked back.

Around the time of my tenth birthday, the Lord told my parents to leave California, pack up their family with all of their belongings, and move us to Texas to start a church. Like Abraham, they obeyed without question. My parents' heart and love for the Lord are extremely real in that way. Their love is physically manifested in everything they say and do.

Unfortunately, for most of my life, I chose to not follow their example. Being raised as a pastor's kid (notoriously known as a "PK"), I was given a lot of head knowledge when it came to spiritual matters, but I did not have a personal relationship with the Lord. I could talk the talk, but I did not want to walk the walk. My parents also started a Christian school which I attended for eight years. This school did not cause me to grow or mature in my love for the Lord because I did not even know what it meant to be in love with anyone but myself. Like the apostle Paul before his conversion, I knew a lot about the scriptures and the law, but I did not personally know the Author. I too, would have to be knocked off my proverbial horse before I would come to know Him as my Lord, Master, Savior, and King.

Like Jonah, I ran as far away as I could to get away from the Lord and His calling on my life. At the age of twenty, I dropped out of college and joined the Navy; thus, I began my service as a member of the Navy's elite Special Operation Units, otherwise known as the SEAL Teams. For the first seven years of my service, I built a kingdom for myself by putting everything into it I had ever desired. I found a beautiful wife, got married, and had two children. I had a job few men could boast of and many men envied. For me, the best part about this kingdom was that I had built it all on my own, without any help from the Lord or my parents. I was the king of my kingdom, and no one could ever take that away from me.

Fortunately, God had other plans for my life. Those plans would remain a mystery to me until I was able to realize and admit my dependency upon Him. In His wisdom and mercy, He allowed the kingdom I had built to crumble down around me. Through a series of events that were brought on by a life lived in sin, I lost everything I had. I was able to remain a Navy SEAL, but I was transferred to a new duty location. I could have been sent to any duty location throughout the world; instead, I was sent back to my hometown Conroe, Texas. It was as though the whale had spit me back up onto the beach right where the Lord wanted me to be all along. Like Jonah, I was not placed on that beach until I had repented for my life of sin and disobedience to the Lord.

Amazingly enough, the same merciful Lord who allowed my kingdom to crumble and fall, also returned my life to me seven-fold. I not only had my family back, but now they were serving the Lord as well. He had put me in an environment where I could grow in Him and learn to love Him the way that He had loved me. I now only wanted to get to know the Father I had spent my life escaping from.

The first lesson He taught me was the lesson of obedience. It had been my disobedience and rebellion that had led me away from Him. This was a vital lesson I had to learn, so the Lord would be able to use me the way He had always planned.

For the next three years, I served in my father's church while learning to love the Lord and listen to His voice. The Lord had been waiting for me to get to know Him for years. Now that I had returned, He wanted to share Himself with me, so He did. By gaining an understanding of who He was, I would better be able to share Him with others by using my own personal experiences rather than just the experiences of others. I was being taught my place within the Kingdom of God, and I was learning to make my love for Him my basis for my motivation to obey Him in all I said and did.

At the end of three years, I was given an opportunity by the Lord to take a step of faith and obey His voice. The Lord asked me to end my service in the Navy, giving up my position as a Navy SEAL, a position which I had held for ten years. This move also meant I had to give up a retirement that was only ten years away. The decision was quite simple for me, actually. After ten years of service and at the age of thirty, I left the job that had been my identity for one-third of my life, not knowing what God had in plan for me and my family.

I felt like Abraham, when he was asked by the Lord to move his household to a place of unknown destination. All I knew was that I wanted to be obedient to the calling of God in my life. I worked in a couple of different jobs over the next few years, all the while trying to serve as much as possible in my parents' church. I was leading my family in a life lived by faith without fully knowing what the Lord had in store for us.

At one point, my wife and I decided to move to Arizona where she could be closer to her mother. I made the decision to move to Arizona, based only upon what I believed the Lord wanted my family to do at the time. I gave up a good job, working for NASA as a safety diver in their Neutral Buoyancy Laboratory. It was my job to look after the astronauts as they trained in a gigantic underwater facility. This training facility helped prepare the astronauts for the rigors of working in a weightless environment. It gave them endurance for their long space walks outside the shuttle and space station. Working with the astronauts was exciting to say the least, but living for God in perfect obedience requires great faith, and this kind of lifestyle is more exciting than anything this world has to offer. Looking back at my decision, I can see why

He asked me to go to Arizona, but at the time, it was all based on faith.

I spent about three months in Arizona, unemployed. I could not understand why I was having such trouble finding a job. I felt like I had a fairly impressive resume, but I could not find anyone to hire me. I began to feel doubt creeping in. When it looked like I was finally going to get a job with the U.S. Border Patrol, the Lord asked us to move back to Texas. I know now He did not want me to be planted there; instead, He was using the time to teach me how to grow in faith and in my devotion to Him.

Before we left Arizona to move back to Texas, I felt like the Lord told me He wanted me to finish the college education I had started fifteen years earlier. At the age of thirty-four, I moved back into my parents' home but this time with my wife and two children. It was a humbling experience to say the least. After all, I use to be a Navy SEAL and the king of a kingdom. I felt like the prodigal son returning home; or at least, my parents treated me as such. They did everything but "kill the fatted calf." They are truly the most loving parents I could have ever hoped for.

When I told them I felt like the Lord was asking me to go back to school full-time, they did not hesitate to offer me everything they had to aid me in my quest. It was not merely a quest of regaining a lost education but a quest of seeking to live in perfect obedience to the Lord. My parents realized that this world and all that it contains, serves only as a work place where we can serve the Father and His Kingdom, preparing ourselves for His Son's return. It is a place where our lives can be used to bring Him glory through our obedience to Him.

When my father left his new CPA practice in California, it was just beginning to become lucrative. They sold their home, moved to Texas, and left behind any financial security they had in this world. For the next few years as their church grew, they lived off of their savings and the money they had made by selling their house, trusting the Lord to make ends meet whenever the finances got tight. I witnessed the Lord work many financial miracles for our family during those lean years. Because of their example, I was inspired to take great leaps of faith in my own life when it came to trusting the Lord.

Towards graduation, I was uncertain of what I would be doing, but I knew the Lord would guide me when the time came. I spent the summer with my wife and children, finding myself wondering again why I could not find work. It was at this point that someone from my past called me. He asked me if I would like a job. The Lord had opened a door, and I found myself accepting a position with a company working in Iraq. It was 2004, and the war against terrorism was in full bloom. I knew immediately it was the Lord, but I did not know why. Personally, I did not want to go, those closest to me did not want me to go, and I knew others within the Church were saying it was not the Lord's will. A few even said that I might be doing it for selfish reasons—namely, the money.

Since that time, I have had people in my own congregation ask me to forgive them for the accusations they made against me. At the time, they did not fully understand why I was making the decision to go, but the Lord had showed them the truth within their own heart. They understood that I only wanted to be obedient to the Lord, and they supported me in my decision to obey God's voice. God had kept His promise to honor those who honor Him.

I had lived my life in disobedience and selfishness, but I was not about to let the Lord down again. My wife and children knew of my heart's desire to obey the Lord, and if I felt like the Lord wanted me to go, they would be obedient to His call as well. It was an easy decision but also a painful one because I had grown accustomed to being at home with my family. I knew from past experience that it would be painful being away from them, especially for one whole year. In another act of blind faith, I left for Iraq.

The Lord used my time in Iraq to show me many things about my personal relationship with Him. I learned many things about the Holy Spirit that I believe were best learned by traveling to Iraq. I have traveled the world many times over, but this was the first time I have been to a Muslim nation as a follower of Christ. During my stay in Iraq, the Lord began to put a burden on my heart to write this book. I have felt this burden many times before, but I knew back then it was not God's timing. He was just giving me a glimpse of things to come.

During the last seven years, the Lord has taught me many things about my relationship with Him and with others in the Body of Christ. Sometimes, He asks me to share with others what He has shown me, but more often than not, He has asked me to wait. I can usually tell if He wants me to wait rather than share. It is more of a compulsion than a desire. I feel that I need to share it, not merely that I want to share it.

Occasionally, I will read an article or book that was written by someone who has similar interests in the Kingdom of God as I do, or I might speak with someone who has had a similar experience with the Lord as I have. Many times these meetings seem to be divinely appointed, and my passion to go deeper with the Lord is fueled even more. It seems that these divine appointments occur just at the right moments in my life to spur me on in my desire to understand Him and His plans for my life. I believe the Lord is opening these doors to bring me closer, to keep me on the path that He has chosen for my life, and to keep me within His perfect timing.

Like I said before, I have felt like writing this book many times since I have been saved, but it is only now that I have been able to do so. It is only now that I feel a compulsion to write it. If I had written this book earlier, it would not have had the same effect because the timing would have been off. I am not exactly sure how the Lord will use my trip to Iraq to benefit the Kingdom, but I am very confident that He gave me the order to go. When the Lord commands me to do something, He rarely tells me why, and I almost never ask. It is not until afterwards that I realize why He wanted me to do it. The Lord has taught me to do His bidding, trusting in Him to guide me through it. It is a wonderful thing when we obey our God and see His plans come to fruition! It is out of this obedience that I have finally been able to put my pen to paper.

I believe the great end time move of the Holy Spirit is approaching rapidly. I also feel there are or will be very soon, key individuals within the Body of Christ who will usher in this visitation. These individuals are known as "forerunners" because they will be the first to operate under this new anointing of grace. Although they will be the first, they will not be the last to experience this new grace. This move of the Holy Spirit will bring the Church into a perfect unity with the Father. It will birth a perfect love in the heart of the Bride of Christ, and it will, in turn, unleash a desire for her to live in perfect obedience to her Master's call. I believe the mature Bride of Christ will eventually arise from within this movement, and soon after, the King will return for her.

I will attempt to identify these forerunners by comparing them with the U.S. military's Special Operation Units. These two groups have many things in common when it comes to their gifts and talents. The service they perform is also very similar in nature. I see specific character traits that are common in both groups and are needed to perform the duties of their specific service. I believe this team of forerunners will be continuously joined by other members of the Body of Christ until a mature Bride of Christ emerges, filling the role of the end time Church. This mature Bride of Christ will be made up entirely of members operating under this new grace. They will be perfect in love, perfect in obedience, and perfect in unity.

Towards the end of my military career, I spent a few years as a Navy SEAL recruiter. I tried to find and enlist highly motivated and extremely gifted young men to serve as Navy SEALs within the U.S. military. I do not feel that it is a coincidence that I would feel called to serve in this role again. One major difference now is that I am recruiting for the King of Kings, instead of man. We have an information pamphlet in the Navy, the "BUD/S Warning Order," handed out to every candidate who desires admittance to BUD/S training. It describes what the training will be like, what can be expected, and how a candidate can prepare for it. This book will play a similar role in preparing the Church for this end time move of the Spirit. Unlike the "BUD/S Warning Order," this information can be utilized by everyone serving in the Kingdom of God, not just the forerunners. I believe the Church is heading to a place of maturity in the Lord that we as a body have yet to witness. We will be led by these forerunners, but we will also be joining them on the field of battle.

The information within this book is based upon lessons I have learned and experiences I have gained while serving as a U.S. Navy SEAL. The spiritual insights are based upon lessons I have learned and experiences I have gained in my personal walk with the Lord and while serving Him within the Church. These words should not be read as scripture because they are not the inspired Word of God. They should be taken exactly for what they are: my own personal views based upon my life's experiences, my interpretation of scripture, and my personal insights into the Spirit given to me by my Lord and Savior. I pray wisdom will be granted to the reader when judging this book, and if this book sparks a fire in the heart of the reader, I pray that the Lord God Himself will fan the flame and divinely reveal His Truth.

Chapter I

A Common Thread

Ten years of my life were spent serving this country as an elite member of the U.S. Navy SEAL Teams. My tour of duty included serving as a SEAL operator, instructing SEALs in the art of combat diving, and promoting the SEAL imagine as a SEAL recruiter. During those ten years, I began to notice common threads of character that seemed to bind us all together. It was as if we were all cut from the same piece of fabric or were all pieces of furniture made from the same tree. It is the type of character that we are born with, not the type of character we gain through life's experiences.

It really became evident to me as I began working as a SEAL recruiter. I watched those young men I enlisted as they attempted to graduate from Basic Underwater Demolition School, arguably the hardest military training in the world. I began to notice a similarity among those who graduated as opposed to those who did not. Getting to know them before they went into the military gave me a different perspective of a SEAL candidate than I had previously been privy to. I began to see in them characteristics that I also had before I went into the military. I then realized these characteristics were common among members of the SEAL community, but they were lacking among those that attempted and failed to achieve that status.

Basic Underwater Demolition School, or more affectionately known as BUD/S, is a six month school that all SEAL candidates must pass through before they can be assigned to a SEAL command. If they are fortunate enough to make it through BUD/S, they are assigned to a SEAL command where they undergo an advanced three month training cycle. They must also pass a strenuous oral and written exam before they are finally awarded the much coveted Trident insignia (a pin worn by all SEALs identifying them as such).

As a SEAL recruiter, I began to notice that those candidates who made it through BUD/S were individuals who had already possessed certain character traits given to them at birth. The demanding training just brought to the surface these gifts that were usually buried within them. Candidates without these traits were easily "washed out" of the training. Very few Navy candidates ever qualify for BUD/S training, and even fewer BUD/S candidates graduate.

BUD/S class 175, my BUD/S class, began its training during the winter of 1990. I would become a member of this class for the next six months. We formed up with ninety-five energetic, confident, and highly motivated candidates. Each one of us knew, beyond a shadow of doubt, we would be there in the end. Unfortunately, BUD/S had other plans in store for us. In the end, six months later, only twelve of the original ninety-five souls still remained.

On average, the attrition rate for BUD/S is seventy percent. There was no reason for those who did not make it through with us to feel ashamed. They all went on to serve in important roles within the regular Navy. They just did not have these identifying character traits, or they were less fortunate and fell to some serious injury that would not allow them to continue. If they did come up short because of a debilitating injury, they were allowed the opportunity to heal and try again, but if they quit or were removed by the instructor staff for any other reason, they were not allowed to return.

These character traits are not written in stone, and I do not claim ownership to some secret formula for success, but the traits I saw in my fellow SEALs are undeniable. These traits are ones of inner character rather than outward physical attributes. Yes, there are physical qualifications that must be met in order to qualify a candidate to gain admittance to BUD/S, and there are physical requirements that must be met in order to graduate, but the all important drive and motivation comes from within, this inner character.

When I went to BUD/S, I did not have the "so-called" physical appearance of a Navy SEAL. Actually, I was quite the opposite. I weighed 135 pounds soaking wet and stood at about 5'10." I was laughed at by my Navy recruiter when I told him I wanted to become a SEAL, and it was hard for me to find anyone who would support me in my decision. My brother Shane was one of the few people in my life who believed in me enough to tell me I had made a good decision. I would soon learn though, my inner drive and determination were worth their weight in gold. My physical abilities played a much smaller role in graduating than I had first anticipated, and my physical appearance played no role at all.

I believe the armies that are fighting within the realm of the spirit are structured and governed very similarly to the armies who are dwelling in the physical world. Events occurring in the spiritual realm are affected by events occurring in the natural and vice versa.

In the Book of Daniel, Daniel was praying and fasting after having been given a vision from the Lord. The Lord heard his prayers and sent a messenger who was not of this earth for encouragement, but the messenger was held up by the Prince of Persia. The Prince of Persia was a demonic spirit that governed the kingdom of Persia. It was Daniel's prayers and fasting that allowed Michael, one of the princes of the Kingdom of God, to be sent to help the messenger to break through the enemies' lines of defense. We are enlisted into the Army of God when we give our lives to Him, and we too become a part of this spiritual war that is constantly raging around us.

Revelations 19:11–19 describes the return of the King of Kings to the earth along with His army. At this time, it explains how the beast and the kings of the earth, along with their armies, will assemble to wage war with the King of Kings. This final battle will be between those who have eternal bodies and those who are mortal. Those who can not die will be fighting against those who can. The end result seems fairly obvious. The King is coming back with His army as a conqueror, so we may dwell with Him in peace forever. Since our world today is obviously not at peace, then we must still be at war.

Our enemy is not of this world, but it is of the spirit. For this reason, in the Kingdom of God we wear armor and use weapons that are not visible to the naked eye. Ephesians 6:10–17 speaks of us putting on the full armor of God in order to be able to stand firm against the devil. It goes on to tell us that our enemy is not made of flesh and blood like ourselves, but it is of the spirit, and it lives in the heavenly places. It will be the King of Kings, along with His returning army, who will finally bring peace to this world by conquering not only the kings of the earth but all evil and banishing it from His kingdom once and for all. Until then we must prepare the world for His return by battling the spiritual forces talked about in Ephesians 6:10–17. They seek to destroy those who now serve or would serve the King of Kings and Lord of Lords.

In the world today, there are many people who do not follow Christ but who still believe in a spiritual realm or existence that is somehow closely connected to our physical world. Just look at all the movies coming out of Hollywood. Hollywood produces films that they know will sell. Our physical minds have a hard time comprehending what the realm of the spirit might be like. The natural desire to understand this spiritual world is why people flood the movie theatres when these types of films are showing. The existence of ghosts, demons, angels, and other spiritual entities is taught through out the world by many different religions. In some parts of the world, it is widely accepted by the general populace as simply being a fact of life. There are even classes being taught within our own universities that discuss spirituality and the afterlife. Most people around the world who believe in a spiritual world also believe we can interact with it. We can see this interaction displayed in the Bible every time Jesus or His disciples spoke to or cast out a demon from some possessed man, woman, or child.

Throughout history we can see that armies have been structured generally in the same way even though they might evolve slightly to keep pace with the weaponry and tactics of the day. For example, cavalry units have been around for thousands of years, but today they fly helicopters instead of riding horses. Armies have always had some type of rank structure from the generals down to the foot soldiers. We see intelligence gatherers all the way back in the Old Testament. Moses sent out twelve spies into the land of Canaan to gather intelligence on the indigenous populace to help better prepare for the upcoming battle.

Today's intelligence gatherers, better known as Special Operation Teams, are used for the same purpose. I do not think it is a coincidence that a SEAL platoon is also made up of twelve members. One tactical reason for having this many members on a team is that a twelve man platoon can be broken into two squads, four fire teams, or six dive teams. Depending upon the nature of a mission, a platoon commander would have the ability to conform his platoon into the necessary size in order to be as effective as possible. For example, if a platoon was going through a highly visible area, they might break up into smaller units to avoid becoming detected. Two men would be able to move more quickly and more quietly than twelve. They would also be able to cover more area and in less time.

The twelve spies who went into the land of Canaan probably came across this situation as well. I would not be surprised if Joshua and Caleb were both teamed up together when they crossed the Jordan. They probably fed off each other's enthusiasm, never hearing the negativity from the other spies until they debriefed Moses and the rest of the children of Israel.

The Lord told Moses to send in these twelve spies. It was His idea, a plan from the greatest Warrior of all and Creator of all things. Since He created this plan of action then there should be an example of it in heaven. He not only has an army of angels in heaven doing battle with the spirits of darkness, but He also has us—the Army of God—in the earth. It would be a rational conclusion to assume that His angelic army and His army here on earth would be structured similarly and use the same kind of tactics He put forth to the children of Israel. There are a few references in the Bible that speak of the things of this world as being a shadow of the things to come or those things that are in heaven. Heaven's angelic army and the army of the saints of God work closely together. The Army of God in the earth shadows those forces that are fighting in the spirit.

It is in this connection between the spiritual and physical that I lay the ground work for what I believe are Special Operation Teams (S.O.T.) in the Army of God. It is my further belief that there are a few of us who will be serving in these S.O.T. Teams in the last days as forerunners to a great move of the Holy Spirit in the Church.

In the military today, we must meet certain physical standards in order to qualify for the service. Likewise, the physical blood of Jesus is what qualifies us for service in His army. All we must do is say "yes" to the Lord and join His army.

Once a candidate has enlisted in the U.S. military, they become eligible to pursue different jobs within the service. As long as they meet the minimum qualifications for a specific job, they will be given an opportunity to pursue it. The character within them, or the lack of character, will either cause them to succeed or fail. God has many different jobs within His army as well, and He has given each of us the inner character needed to succeed at the specific job He has created us for.

The scriptures says in 1 Corinthians,

> "And God has appointed in the church, first apostles, second prophets, third teachers, then miracles, then gifts of healings, helps, administrations, various kinds of tongues" (1 Corinthians 12:28).

It goes on to say these gifts are for the perfecting of the saints. When this perfecting is complete, we will no longer need these gifts to be given out individually or separate of each other because we will all be able to perform whatever action is necessary in order to accomplish God's will. This is where the Church is heading as it becomes the mature Bride of Christ.

In today's military, if a candidate joins the Navy to pursue a career as a Navy SEAL, only to find it is not their calling, they still remain in the Navy. They just have to refocus on a different job until they find one they are successful at. There are counselors along the way to help us plan for success by focusing our attention on a job that we have the character or skills for. In God's army, if we attempt to answer this higher calling, only to find out it is not our specific calling at this time, we still remain in God's army. We also have counselors known as pastors who can help guide us to the position God has enabled us for.

There is no shame in trying to hear from the Lord, being obedient to His voice, and only then finding out we missed the mark. If we believe God wants us to do something, and we pursue that course but find out we are going about it all the wrong way, we only have to change our direction slightly, and we will still end up on target. In the SEAL Teams, we would say "adapt and overcome." God is faithful to guide His servants when their desire is one of obedience to Him. I have been on many missions in the Seal Teams where the best intelligence available told us what we should expect, only to find out we were sorely misled.

About ten years ago, I took part in a training exercise in South Korea. The purpose of this exercise was to test the security forces on a few South Korean and U.S. military bases along the coast. Sometimes, SEALs are called upon to try to breach the security on U.S. bases, so the base commanders might learn of any weaknesses in their defenses.

On this particular mission, we were given orders to penetrate the outer security forces, move to a position to fire simulated rockets at a water tower, and then extract to our pick up point. We had to do all of this without becoming detected or captured. One of my positions within the platoon was point man. As point man I was responsible for planning the insertion and extraction for the mission. In other words, I had to find us a way in and a way out without getting caught.

This same security breaching mission had also been given to twenty-one other Special Operation Units in the area that were taking part in the exercise. We were given a window of seven days in which we could attack the base, and we had about two to three days to plan for it. I gathered all the intelligence I could find, and devised a plan that I thought would give us the best opportunity for success. The intelligence was pretty good. I had photos of the base and the surrounding area, enemy patrol information, and other important data to help in my planning.

On the night of our insertion the weather became extremely cold. Most of my team had not prepared for the weather to drop in temperature as much as it did. Even if we had planned for it, we probably would have still dressed the same. As one of our sayings go, "Travel light, freeze at night!"

The boats we were using for our insertion were having engine trouble, and by the time we got to the first known check point, we were two hours behind schedule. In Korea, the tide changes are pretty dramatic, so what should have been three to four feet of water two hours before, was now dry land. Our boats hit dry land about one mile out from the beach.

We were forced to make some radical changes if we were to complete this mission successfully. My lieutenant decided to only take what was absolutely necessary—basically, the weapons and ammunition we usually carried and the rockets. We left a security element with the boats and took off.

Because we were so far out and so far behind in time, we decided to run. It was dark, rainy, cold and windy. Just the kind of weather we like to work in. Nobody in their right mind would venture out into this weather, including those guards who would be looking for us. We made up about thirty minutes on our run. The quick jaunt also helped to warm us up.

When we got to the fence line, we began to move much slower. Staying low to the ground, I moved to a place where I could get a better look around. Everything was just as it should be according to the intelligence. I led the way as we crawled along through an irrigation ditch in a field next to the base's outer perimeter fence line.

When we got to within one hundred and fifty feet of the perimeter fence I noticed a concrete wall running parallel to the fence line. In front of the wall was a dirt road. I had not seen this road or wall on any of the intelligence reports I had been given prior to the mission planning. It was in our way though, and there was no way to go around it. I quickly decided to cross the road and go over the wall. Giving a nod to my lieutenant and keeping as low as possible, I quickly crossed the road and jumped over the wall. I really should have looked before I jumped. What appeared to be a two foot wall from the other side of the road now turned into a ten foot deep concrete sewer line used for the base. I had managed to jump into one of the open sections of the sewer line and into about five feet of waste. Standing there in chest deep sewage, I wondered what my buddies would say when they came over the wall.

It actually was a blessing in disguise. No one would be looking for us in the sewer lines, and they did not have any defenses set up inside of them either. We were able to use the sewer line to infiltrate the base, destroy the target, and get back out safely.

By making a few modifications to our insertion plans, I was able to help my team complete the mission. Out of the twenty one units, we were the only unit to successfully complete the mission. During the debriefing, the base commander could not believe we had used the sewer lines. Using the information provided by our platoon, the base commander was able to upgrade the base defenses. Sometimes in life we must adapt to situations going on around us if we are going to be successful in what we are doing. The same can be said when we are trying to obey God.

In the SEAL community, our physical appearance plays no part in either qualifying us for BUD/S training or in helping us to get through it. Ironically, a SEAL platoon will be made up of twelve men who do have much in common when it comes to their physical appearance. They all seem to dress the same when they are off duty, even down to the type of sandals they wear on their feet. Basically, they all have the same body type because of their line of work and the physical training they all go through. Of course, the military makes sure they all have the same kind of haircut. If each individual member of a platoon walked into a crowded room at different times, it would be fairly easy to identify them as being together. Much of it has to do with the way they carry themselves, but the more they are around each other, the more they become like each other. They become brothers; they become family.

God's S.O.T. Teams are no different. Worldly and physical appearances will not be taken into consideration when we are applying for this special service, and they definitely will not help us when the trials begin. We do not have to be a television evangelist, a pastor of some large congregation, or have some other noticeable ministry to qualify. We do not even have to be a pastor's son or daughter or have been saved for a long period of time in order to make this type of a commitment. I do believe that those who choose to serve in God's S.O.T. Teams will be easily recognized by the world. Because they will have so much of the Holy Spirit living within them, He will even change their physical countenance. Remember when Moses came off the top of Mt. Sinai? The scriptures say his face shined like the sun because of all the time he had spent in the presence of God. God's S.O.T. Team members will begin to look more like Christ, not in their physical attributes, but in the outward manifestation of the Holy Spirit in their lives. They will talk the same, act the same, and even appear to others to look the same outwardly. The more they are around others within the Church, the more the Church will begin to look like Christ as well. Pretty soon, the world will begin to notice a difference between themselves and the Body of Christ.

In the SEAL Teams, we prefer candidates who do

not have any preconceived notions concerning the job because we can teach them the way we want them to do things without having to fight bad habits they might have picked up along the way. I believe this is one reason why Jesus chose tax-gatherers, doctors, and fisherman for His disciples. This does not mean that God can not use a pastor's son who was raised in a church for most of his life. At least, I hope not. My father has been a pastor since I was ten years old. The apostle Paul was also a rabbi, but by his own account he was a murderer because of his persecution of the early Christians.

My point is that God does not choose someone for this particular kind of service because of what they have done. He chooses them because of who they are, and what He has put into them. My mother received a word from the Lord about me years ago. He told her He was going to "get out of me what He had put into me". It was meant as a word of encouragement for her because at the time I was not serving the Lord. Since then, I have given my life to Him, and I have found myself clinging to that word through many hard times in my life. I have found myself staring into a mirror and telling myself out loud, "It does not matter what is going on around you just keep on believing because the Lord has promised to get out of you what He has put into you!"

I believe this word is for the Body of Christ today. We all have gifts of character that the Lord has given us. I also believe He gave them to us for a purpose. Regardless of who we are or where we have been, He will get out of us what He has put into us! There is a common thread running through those that are called to these S.O.T. Teams, and it is my prayer that by the end of this book it will become self evident in the lives of those who have been chosen for this service.

The following four chapters deal with common character traits found in both the U.S. Special Operation Units, and in God's Special Operation Teams. These traits are innate and can not be taught or learned to any great extent.

Chapter II

The Extremist Within

As far back as I can remember, I have always enjoyed a good challenge. I especially enjoy a challenge where there is the potential for great gain as well as great loss. Growing up, my friends and I would build ramps to jump our bikes over. We would place cardboard boxes and other items behind the ramp to make the jump more difficult. I was the type of kid who would have to light those items on fire before making the jump. My actions were not simply to show off for my friends but were meant to make the jump as challenging as possible. I wanted there to be consequences if I failed. I have participated in combat night jumps out of a plane, climbed snow covered mountains during white out conditions, and swam at night with sharks off the coast of Africa. Some might think these actions are the actions of a mad man, but I prefer to be labeled as an "extremist."

What is an extremist? Webster's Dictionary defines the word extreme as, "very great or intense; something located at one end or the other of a range." These are intense individuals. Usually, living most of their lives on one end or the other in everything they think, say, and do. Extremism definitely involves pushing the outer limits of what many believe to be possible. It does not always involve a physical challenge either. Many extremists can be found today in the area of politics and religion. I am reminded of an American patriot named Patrick Henry. He showed an extreme approach to freedom when he said, "Give me freedom or give me death!" A compromise was not acceptable. In just about any area where ideals are expressed, someone can be found who will hold to some extreme point of view. In fact, when someone attempts something so challenging that it is labeled as "extreme", their point of view will usually play a very large role in their success or failure.

An extremist does not act on insane impulses, but rather on calculated risk assessment. We must train, prepare, and plan so that when the time comes, we are confident in our abilities to pull it off. This confidence comes from having a sound understanding of the facts involved, along with a thorough understanding of the consequences for failure.

Think about space travel for a moment. Imagine strapping into a seat on top of a rocket filled with millions of gallons of highly combustible fuel. This rocket is then shot into space to land on the moon. Upon returning to earth, it crash lands into the ocean. If I would have mentioned space travel to someone just a few hundred years ago, they would have had me locked up in an insane asylum. Because of advancements in science and technology, we have now come to realize that space travel is, in fact, quite possible. Is it dangerous? Yes. Are astronauts crazy? Absolutely not! Actually, they are some of the most intelligent people on this planet; however, these intelligent people do push the limits on what we believe we are capable of as humans.

So why do people believe something is impossible one day but totally possible the next? The answer is faith. Many people today put their faith in science and technology. When science tells them something is possible they believe it. People look to science and technology to solve most of their everyday problems. When Christopher Columbus sailed across the ocean, science told him he would fall off the end of the earth because it was flat. A few of his peers might have labeled him as an extremist, but most of the public called him crazy. Think of what the world would be like today if he had never sailed across the Atlantic. Maybe someone else would have done it eventually, but then again, maybe not.

We also find ourselves believing in new possibilities when we witness someone else doing things we once thought were impossible. Case in point, the first time the four minute mile was broken. Scientists once believed that it was impossible for the human body to run one mile in under four minutes. They believed the human heart could not withstand that kind of strain. Roger Bannister, a British collegiate runner and medical student, believed in himself more than he believed in the medical doctors of his time and banished all disbelief when he became the first man to ever accomplish this feat. Today, even high school students have run under four minute miles. When someone does the impossible, others begin to see the possibilities.

The extremist lives on the edge of a cliff. The ground under their feet is what society is willing to accept as being possible. As they take a step off into the void, society witnesses what we are truly capable of. What makes it possible for the extremist to go where others fear to tread? It is simply that their faith comes from a different source.

The extremist is usually the first one to experience the unknown. I would definitely classify Navy SEALs as having an extremist personality. SEALs are one of the first groups to be called in when there is an unknown danger that needs to be identified. They are the eyes and ears for the Command and Control in the field. If an Admiral wants to know what kind of threat awaits his landing force, he will send in a SEAL platoon under the cover of darkness to gather intelligence. The more difficult the mission, the more likely a SEAL platoon will be utilized. If it looks impossible then we want the job. This is neither the act of crazy men, nor is it simply bravado. It is a calculated decision based upon risk assessment. By using the known intelligence of the area, the experience of the platoon, training, and planning, we can establish a course of action that we can be confident in.

Extremism is all or nothing. I have friends who are always telling me, "Beau, you are such an extremist!" My wife Eva would be the first to tell you that whatever I do I put my all into it or not at all. Extremist tend to be narrow minded but not in a negative way. Usually, we are so focused on the task at hand that everything else around us gets put into the background of our mind until we are ready or need to focus on it once again.

I have felt a strong desire to be back in the SEAL Teams many times since I have left the military. Why? It was a period of my life when I had to live on the edge of the unknown. I had to put my life on the line many times in my service to this country. That kind of lifestyle is not lived today by the average person in American society. I would be hard pressed to find somewhere that I could fit in where I would have to place myself in that same position again. There are jobs that require that kind of commitment, but they are few and far between.

I worked for NASA for about a year as a safety diver at the Neutral Buoyancy Laboratory in Houston, Texas. I had to protect the lives of the astronauts as they practiced space walks in a huge pool used to simulate a space environment. We would weigh them out so their weight would be neutral in the water, putting them in an environment as close as possible to that of space. Every training scenario was a matter of life or death. At any time, something could happen that would demand an immediate response from the safety divers to ensure the safety of the astronauts. I had the opportunity to work with extremists as they trained for a job that required every ounce of energy and focus they could muster.

I always thought I had a problem with being a quitter as I was growing up. I had a dream when I was younger of becoming a professional triathlete. I even took a year off after high school to pursue my dream. All I did everyday was prepare by body and mind in the hopes that I might accomplish my dream. I made tremendous advancements that year, and at the end of the season I had reached my goal. There were only a few more races I wanted to do as an amateur before I would turn professional.

It was during one of these races that the worst thing imaginable happened to me. I sustained a serious injury to my right knee. My season was over and so were my dreams. For the next few months, I watched as my competitors got faster, and I faded away. My mind had been so focused on becoming a professional triathlete, I had not allowed myself to see anything else.

When I became injured, my mind began to wander. I began to look for something that I could focus my attention on again. My energy and enthusiasm began to pool up until I felt like I was going to go crazy if I did not find something worthy of my time and efforts. Eventually, I decided to go to college to pursue a collegiate career in swimming.

Some might say I quit on my dream of becoming a professional triathlete, and at that time, I would have agreed with them. Since then, I have learned that my extremist personality demands my complete and undivided attention to one goal at a time. I must be able to feel I am giving everything I have, or it is not worth doing. If I lose the ability to give my all, I must find something else that I can pursue.

With the war on terrorism raging and cult groups abounding, the word "extremist" has taken on a negative connotation, but this should not be the case. Extremism, in and of itself, is not a negative word. Like with everything God has created, Satan has tried to use extremism to his advantage. If we live an extreme lifestyle that is contrary to the Word of God then we live in extreme sin. It is the sin that is negative, not the extreme lifestyle. The Bible says it best in Revelations when the Lord says,

> "I know your deeds, that you are neither cold nor hot; I wish that you were cold or hot. So since you are lukewarm, and neither hot nor cold, I will spit you out of My mouth" (Revelations 3:15–16).

God wants us to be extreme! He wants us to be extremely in love with Him. Do not just be hot, but be scalding hot! I want to be living my life on the verge of spontaneous combustion in my pursuit to love the Lord with every fiber of my being!

The Bible is full of examples of individuals who were extremists because of their extreme faith. Hebrews

11 speaks of a few of them. Abraham gave up everything to follow a God he had never seen and to go to a place he had never been. He was even going to offer up his only son, Isaac, as a burnt offering to the Lord out of obedience to his God. Fortunately, the Lord stopped him, but even if He had not, Abraham believed that God would have brought Isaac back from the dead. This faith is evident when he told his servant that both he and his son would return together after they had gone to offer their sacrifice to the Lord. Samson took the Nazarite vow; an oath to the Lord that was considered extreme, even by many who walked the earth at that time. David did not walk, but ran to fight Goliath! There are also those men in Hebrews:

> They were stoned, they were sawn in two, they were tempted, they were put to death with the sword; they went about in sheepskins, in goatskins, being destitute, afflicted, ill-treated, (men of whom the world was not worthy), wandering in deserts and mountains and caves and holes in the ground. (Hebrews 11:37–38)

I am sure there are people in the world today who have been compelled to live their lives like these radical men. In some places of the world, they have.

Jesus, the most radical extremist ever, lived a life without sin in complete obedience to the Father and died on the cross to deliver mankind from eternal damnation! Just imagine the Father for a moment . . . He is God . . . He is the Creator of all things, including time, space, and laws. What would be the most extreme act of compassion and mercy our Father could show to His children? How about offering His Son to die a humiliating and painful death? He chose this method because He wanted to show

His extreme love for His children. He did not have to offer us salvation for our sins.

When Jesus went to the cross, His actions were not based on irrational thought, but instead, they were founded in the faith He had in His Father. What gave Him the strength to do something no man had ever done before? His faith did not come from His own abilities or His knowledge about science. His faith came from His knowledge of the Father, and Who He was in Him. Jesus knew why He had been born into this world, and He put everything he had into fulfilling that commission. Jesus' ministry lasted only three years, but when we are willing to truly give it our all, there is no wasted time. To give our all means to do anything the Lord asks of us, whenever He asks us to do it. It means to do it to the best of our abilities with joy and love in our hearts.

I believe the Body of Christ today should take advantage of the time that is given to us to prepare for the things that are to come, much like the astronauts I trained with at the Neutral Buoyancy Laboratory. The Body of Christ needs to spend time in training by seeking the Lord in prayer and by studying the Scriptures. We should be dedicating ourselves to the work of the Lord now, during this time of relative peace and security. The world is heating up, and when it turns against us as promised in scripture and begins to persecute the Church globally, we will still be continuing on with our Kingdom duties, only the dangers will be much closer than they are now. We will be working in space, having left the training pool.

To be extreme in these end days we will have to live exactly as Christ. Is God going to entrust the power of the Holy Spirit with someone who would willingly disobey Him? The scripture says, *"And we are witnesses of these things; and so is the Holy Spirit, whom God has given to those who obey Him" (Acts 5:32).* Will He allow them to yield a weapon that could be capable of great destruction if they have sin in their lives? Imagine the devastation if just one nuclear warhead was detonated in any major city around the globe. Would we want the President of the United States to launch a nuclear warhead into Houston, Texas, just to get even with someone? No, of course not. With great power comes great responsibility.

God has always required holiness from those who have worked under a heavy anointing of the Holy Spirit. Many people in the Church today would consider living a life in perfect obedience to the Father as being extreme. Well, they would be correct. Since we are called to live as Christ lived, then let us be extreme! Can we live our lives in perfect obedience to the Father and without sin? I believe we not only can, but we must. Romans 6–8 says we are "*free from the power of sin.*" I will go further into this later on in the book.

First, let us take this extreme approach one step further. Why does the world call us Christians? Where did the use of the word "Christian" originate? Jesus did not call His followers by that name; in fact, He called them His disciples. During the time of the early Church, unbelievers in Antioch first used the Greek name "Christianos" (Χριστιανός) when making reference to those who followed the doctrines and teachings of Jesus Christ. This Greek word was developed from the Greek word "Christos" (Χριστός) meaning "the anointed one." The word originally meant "those who are like Christ." The term "Christianos" is likely to have first been used by a pagan Antioch administration as a designator for a distinct group that was living among the Jewish community in Antioch. The term bore an extremely negative stigma that was felt by all those who were labeled with it. The word did not truly take hold though until the followers of Christ decided to wear it as a badge of honor, giving them a way to join in the sufferings of Christ. I, for one, am tired of hearing the word "Christian" being thrown around today like it is some kind of fraternity. There are all kinds of sinners who claim to be Christians, as if the name alone will keep them out of hell. I am speaking of those who live in sin, are aware of their sin, refuse to repent, yet still call themselves Christian.

Not only the world but also much of the Church today has a misconception of the Body of Christ when it comes to being a Christian. Why do I say this? Webster's 2004 dictionary defines the term as: Christian *n*: adherent of Christianity ~ *adj*: relating to or professing a belief in Christianity or Jesus Christ. Christianity *n*: religion derived from the teachings of Jesus Christ. In other words, a Christian is someone who remains loyal or sticks fast to the teachings of Jesus Christ. In the gospel of Mark when Jesus was asked what the greatest commandment was He said:

> AND YOU SHALL LOVE THE LORD YOUR GOD WITH ALL YOUR HEART, AND WITH ALL YOUR SOUL, AND WITH ALL YOUR MIND, AND WITH ALL YOUR STRENGTH. The second is this, YOU SHALL LOVE YOUR NEIGHBOR AS YOURSELF. There is no other commandment greater than these.

Jesus also said in John 14:15 that if we love Him we will keep His commandments. Are these two commandments being obeyed by Christians today? Were these two commandments being obeyed by the men in the Bible who were described as being, "*men of whom the world's not worthy*?" What is the difference between those individuals and the Christians of today? Our definition today sounds pretty watered down, doesn't it?

In America today, many people believe if they just go to church every Sunday they have earned the right to call themselves a Christian. They believe this allows them to enjoy all of the perks and privileges that go along with carrying that name. It is like having a "get out of hell free card." Attending church every Sunday or even professing that we believe in God is not enough for us to be considered to be like Christ. The Bible says even Satan believes, and when Christ returns, every knee will bow and every tongue will confess that Jesus Christ is Lord. Will this make the devil a Christian? By today's worldly standards he would not be far off.

When someone asks me if I am a Christian, I tell them some people might call me that, but I prefer to see myself as a disciple or follower of Christ. I then go on to explain my reasoning exactly as I have explained it here. For example, while I was a candidate in BUD/S training, I would never have even dreamed of calling myself a Navy SEAL. There are a few people out there today who are claiming to be Navy SEALs, but they have never actually graduated from BUD/S training. No matter what they do or say in the open, I can tell you one thing is for sure; deep down inside they know they are lying.

I believe it is the same within the Church, or at least, will be soon enough. There is coming a day when only true believers will call themselves Christian because that claim will lead to suffering and possibly even death. The Bible says in Acts 5 that the Holy Spirit moved through the apostles in the early Church with so much power that it struck fear into the hearts of all those who heard of it. They stayed away from the apostles because they were afraid of what might happen to them if they came too close. It says further that many were still constantly being added to their number. I believe those who joined them did so with open eyes and came with everything they had.

What about all of the persecution during the early periods of the Church? Back then a Christian had to be ready to die as soon as they gave their lives to the Lord, and I do not mean the spiritual kind of death. Carrying the name of a Christian brought with it the promise of suffering and death. They were more likely to be on the ground level of the Roman Coliseum being fed to the lions than they were to be drinking coffee and chatting with their friends before the Sunday morning service. Do not get me wrong. I love to drink coffee and fellowship with my friends as much as the next believer, but I had better be willing to face the lions if need be. There are many today who have been deceived into believing that they are actually a disciple of Christ. When the persecution and suffering comes, they will quickly find out if their house is built upon sand or upon the Rock.

Until that time, we who are true believers should live our lives in a way that imitates Christ and earns us the title of "Christian." In this way, we might be an example unto the rest of the Church and the even unto the world, so they might see their lives for what they truly are, and then they might truly repent. I know many might be thinking, "There goes Beau again, blowing things way out of proportion! He is always taking everything to such extreme measures!" Well, I am glad to see they are finally getting my point.

When I was in the SEAL teams, I would laugh sometimes when people who were not in our community made comments concerning our training. Do not get me wrong, it was very hard indeed, but I heard things that were unbelievable! They would ask me if I had been drowned on purpose and then resuscitated, allowing me the opportunity to first experience a drowning in a controlled environment before having it happen to me on my own while "on the job." I guess the idea was that I could face a future drowning without fear since I would have already lived through it once. Someone also once asked me if I had been shot on purpose by my instructors while I was at BUD/S. Again, the reasoning was that this would allow us to face the enemy without the fear of the unknown. I could go on and on. I did not mind the stories because anything people said about us just made us seem even more heroic and indestructible. Best of all, our enemies hear these stories and fear us even more. There are examples of this within the Church as well.

There were once seven sons of a Jewish chief priest, considered by many to be exorcists, attempting to battle against demonic forces without the Spirit of God behind them. They approached a man who had a demon and told the demon to come out of the man saying, "In the name of Jesus of whom Paul preaches." It says in Acts,

> "And the evil spirit answered and said to them, 'I recognize Jesus, and I know about Paul, but who are you?'" (Acts 19:15).

When Jesus came up to the demonic man who lived in the graveyard, the demons came pleading to him not to bother them. They were afraid of Him as I am sure they feared Paul. Of course, it was not necessarily Paul they feared: but instead, the One that was working through him that gave him his power. As a SEAL, my enemies did not fear me as an individual, but they feared us as a community or team. Extremists accomplish feats that become legend. The feats grow in size as they are passed down from one generation to the next.

I once heard someone ask, "If your life was a written book would anyone be interested in reading it?" As I pondered this question, I felt like the Lord asked me, "Beau, if your life was read before My throne would I be pleased in hearing it, and would it bring Me glory?" Would our lives bring Him glory? If we can not answer "yes" then we need to make some changes. While we might not all have our lives turned into books or movies here on earth, we will all have our lives read before the throne of God. What will it take to be able to stand before the Lord like it says in Matthew 25:21 and hear Him say, "*Well done my good and faithful servant*?"

In the parable of the talents, Jesus said the servant who hid his one talent in the ground was banished from the master's sight, but the servants who used their talents wisely were honored with more. If God has entrusted us with the character needed to become one of these elite warriors in these end times, then we should step out and go to the extremes in our service to the King!

It has been said, "Nothing ventured, nothing gained." Greater glory will be bestowed upon the King when His servants risk everything for the Kingdom. What glory comes when we are only willing to give up the things we do not really desire? As a SEAL, we must learn to give up our own personal ambitions and desire for personal glory in order to bring all glory and prestige to our community. A SEAL must be willing to put everything on the line every time they step out to go on a mission.

Our lives are not our own, but they belong to those who serve with us. No SEAL has ever been left behind; a motto or creed we all hold dear. It is an extremist point of view, but it has to be that way because of the dangers involved in our kind of work. One of the reasons we are so willing to take on an assignment others might consider too dangerous is because we believe in each other. I know my teammate has my back. Who has our back when we go up against the evil hordes of the enemies of the Lord? It is the King himself. We can draw strength and courage knowing that He will be there right beside us, even within us, as we do battle. We must fully believe this in order to take that step of faith off into the dark abyss. If I had allowed myself to lose my faith in my fellow SEALs at anytime, I would not have been able to do the things I did. The fear that would have gripped me would have been my downfall and could have led to serious injury or even death.

When we are behind the enemy's spiritual lines, a momentary lapse of faith could be our last. Our shield will be lowered, and the enemy could make the deadly blow. This faith is the key to being an extremist for the King in these end times.

I remember a specific mission I went on in Somalia, Africa during Operation Restore Hope. There had been an incident within the city of Mogadishu between American soldiers and warring rebels. Our Black Hawk helicopters had been shot down, and American soldiers had been killed during heavy street fighting. We were called in to provide sniper support and gather intelligence for the American and coalition forces that were operating within the city. We were placed throughout the city on roof tops and towers to keep vigil over the coalition forces and prevent any further rebel uprisings. While operating in four man elements, two of us would sleep and two would stand watch. We were isolated in many of the locations we were placed in, and had minimal defenses established. The only real support we had came from our small team and the air support offered by the C-130 gun ships that flew day and night over head.

While sitting atop a roof in one of these isolated locations, my team was ordered to move to a near-by building in order to evaluate it and to see if it offered a better vantage point for our operation. We woke up our two teammates who were sleeping, so they could give us cover as the two of us moved down the street to the new location. Moving through the streets I felt a growing sense of danger, and I had a strong desire to get back to the security of our roof top. I remember glancing over my shoulder to the location we had just left. I felt quite exposed having no one immediately around us to help in the event of an enemy attack. We were moving during the daylight hours, so we were quite visible to everyone in and around the streets. As we patrolled to the new location which was not very far away, I felt like a hundred sets of eyes were following us. It did not help that every child in the street wanted to come up to us to get candy, food, or whatever we had available to give to them. It was at this very moment of insecurity that I noticed my teammates' .50 caliber sniper rifle pointed from the roof top in our direction. Instantly, this gave me a feeling of security because I knew if anything happened they had my back. We did not fear our enemy. It was our enemy who feared us. What allowed us to walk those streets without being attacked? After all, there were only two of us. The enemy knew we had cover from above. They knew if they tried anything, it would be the last thing they ever did. How did they know this? Snipers in the military have a saying, "One shot, one kill." This reality strikes fear into the heart of the enemy because they realize they will not even have a fighting chance. It will be all over for them before it even starts. They fear the accuracy of the sniper.

Our sniper teams had already shown the enemy what we were capable of, so they knew better than to attempt anything. This sense of security gave us and the other coalition forces working within the city the opportunity to do our job quickly and efficiently. Working in this kind of extreme environment was made possible by the faith we had in ourselves and each other. It also helped that the enemy knew our capabilities and feared us more than we feared them.

God's S.O.T. Teams will also be full of extremists. They will be extreme in their dedication to the King. They will sense fear but will not be afraid. They will have great faith, and they will move mountains. Just as in the days of old, they will be like those "*men of whom the world's not worthy*." In those days, the oppression that the followers of Christ suffered with gave way to great feats of faith. As evil increases in the world, these opportunities will once again present themselves to the Church. Will we be ready?

The fear will not be in us but in our spiritual enemies. Satan and his demons will fear. They will not fear us, but they will fear the Holy Spirit working in us. In Acts 17:6 the apostles were described as, "*men who have upset the world!*" Church, it is time to shake things up again! Spiritual feats will be turned into legends, bolstering the faith of those fellow believers who hear of them and drawing those unbelievers who hear of them into the Kingdom. They will strike fear into the enemy's ranks while bringing glory to our King! When the children of Israel came out of Egypt and journeyed into the Promised Land, the stories of their victories in battle preceded them. The fear of God fell upon those nations who stood in the way of His promises. They did not fear the children of Israel; rather, they feared the God who led them and lived within their midst. This is the time for the Church to arise and take hold of the promises of God once again. The enemies of God will fear the Church and will flee before her presence, not because of the people within it but because of the glory of God that will become evident within her midst.

Chapter III

The Only Easy Day Was Yesterday

Captain John Paul Jones, a patriot in American history, when confronted with surrender or defeat was quoted as saying, "I have not yet begun to fight!" Americans have always been known for their brazen attitudes when standing up for freedom and their inalienable rights. We have been a determined people since the birth of this nation. This determination is a human quality that is given to all of us at birth. Some of us are given more than others, but all of us have it to some extent. It is an innate quality that God gives us, but the enemy tries to silence it at a young age. What drives a baby to learn to walk even after falling time and time again? It is sheer determination.

Why then do some of us seem more driven or determined than others? I believe there are levels of determination reflecting how much of the quality God has given us. Those who have a small quantity are easily crushed by the enemy, while those who have an endless supply of determination pose a greater challenge for the enemy. It can be seen in a child's face when they are determined to accomplish something. Sadly, we can also see it wither away and vanish all together as a parent crushes it to death by telling a child their idea is stupid, or they are wasting their time. The enemy tries to use those who are closest to us to dissuade us from a desire God has placed within our hearts. He knows that a stranger's comments are not as effective as someone whose opinion we hold so dear.

Determination can sometimes be warped into rebellion by the enemy. When an individual's feelings are hurt, the enemy tries to sneak in and deceive the person into believing they are being determined, when actually, they have become rebellious. This will usually occur over time with repeated assaults and almost always when the determination is based upon selfish motives. For those determined in the ways of God, rebellion will not be a factor because God's ways will never lead us to sin. Those who are given large amounts of determination from the Lord and seek His ways are those that seem to thrive in the face of adversity.

As a SEAL candidate, we are constantly faced with adversity from our instructors. They are continually letting us know that we are not good enough to be there, and we will fail if we persist. Throughout much of the training their goal is to persuade us to quit. They are not trying to develop a "loser" mentality in us. Instead, they are trying to find those who do not have the determination needed and wash them out. BUD/S is more of a proving ground than a training facility. We do learn things there, but most of our learning is done when we get to our commands. I have learned the harshness and adversity the instructors represent is far more subtle than what the enemy will unleash on us should we some day find ourselves in a combat environment.

In order to help us prepare our minds for the punishment that lay ahead, we resign ourselves to the fact that we will suffer and there is no getting around it. We have a saying that helps to motivate us, "The only easy day was yesterday!" This might not sound too motivational, but if we go into each day ready to face a more challenging day than the day before then we will not be disappointed. If the day somehow manages to be easier then we are pleasantly surprised. It seems to me that everyday was just as I thought it would be, much harder and more miserable than the day before. By accepting the fact that we will suffer, we identify the need to be highly motivated and determined at all times.

This method of approach teaches us to take each day, one day at a time. If we think too far ahead we will become discouraged because we will see all the hardships awaiting us. If we can just make it through the day we are in, then we will be able to face the next day with renewed vigor and motivation. I personally used the method of just trying to survive until the next hot shower. I knew if I could thaw out for a moment then I could make it a little longer. One hot shower led to the next, and eventually, I found myself graduating from a program that should have killed me.

I remember going through training and deciding I would rather die than admit defeat. I would never utter those hateful words, "I quit!" I knew the instructors were not going to kill me on purpose, or at least, I had hoped not. If somehow during the program I ran across a situation bringing upon my death, then so be it, but I would never quit! This resolve would be tested more than once during my stay at BUD/S.

I remember one time in particular I had to "walk the walk," and not just "talk the talk." It was during the month of February, and the ocean off the coast of California was a chilly 55 degrees. We were learning how to do beach reconnaissance. The training mission called for a night time beach landing, a landing made all the more dangerous by an angry ocean that was just waiting to devour us. The waves were running from about eight to ten feet in height, and there was an extremely strong current. We had to swim into the beach from outside the surf zone while towing behind us our gear, weighing in at over fifty pounds. After we finished the beach survey, we were to swim back out through the surf and meet up with the extraction vessels.

My swim buddy and I took a deep breath and plunged into the freezing cold water (we were not allowed to wear wet suits). The initial shock took our breath away, but we quickly shook it off and began the long swim into the beach. I knew right away we were going to have trouble getting back out because it took us a lot longer to reach the beach than it should have.

By the time we were ready to head back out, I was freezing. It was winter, and the air temperature was in the low 50's. We grabbed our gear, put on our fins and masks, and began the swim back out to the boats. I was so cold the frigid ocean water seemed to warm my frozen limbs. It was extremely dark out because there were no stars or moon in the sky. It was the kind of darkness totally void of any light, and it seemed to rob us of whatever warmth our bodies might have been providing because of our efforts. To top it all off, the waves seemed to take pleasure in pounding us over and over again, always pushing us back in towards the beach.

In BUD/S, every time we were swimming or diving, we always had to have someone with us, so we could keep an eye on each other. In this situation, with this kind of weather, it was almost impossible to stay together. My swim buddy and I were separated almost immediately upon entering the water. I would be lying if I said I did not become at least a little nervous. We wear inflatable life jackets for safety, but if we inflated our jackets in that kind of surf, they would not help us much. They would have just kept us from being able to dive under the waves. We would have gotten pounded by the waves and washed along until the waves let go of us, then we could have finally surfaced for a breath of air.

I had made it about half of the way out when I began to feel the effects of my struggle and the cold. I knew I was running out of time and energy. About three quarters of the way out I started to feel extremely fatigued. I was really worried about cramping, and I knew if I did not get out soon then I might not make it out at all. The pack I was pulling felt like a small car, and it seemed to me the waves had gotten bigger and came at me even more frequently than before. I was having problems keeping myself afloat, and my forward speed had almost come to a complete stop.

I was not living for the Lord at the time, but I did know about the Lord. I seem to remember thinking I might be seeing Him pretty soon and wondering if I should repent. It is sad how many people seem to only call upon the Lord when they are in trouble or when they need something from Him. It is even sadder when someone knows they can call out to Him, but will not because of the hardness of their heart. It is this latter position I found myself in while struggling against the waves, ocean currents, and the cold. Placing all fear and doubt aside,

I gathered every bit of strength I had left and made one last push.

When my needle fell to empty I thought I was done for, and I reached for my life jacket inflation device. Even if I pulled it, I knew I could not survive being washed into the beach because I was so spent at that point I could not hold my breath long enough to survive being hit by another wave. As if I was dreaming, I heard a faint voice. I looked up, saw the extraction boat right next to me, and raised my hand up to be pulled into it. Today, I am sure the Lord had His hand on me, but it was the determination He had put into me that helped me to survive the ordeal.

The Lord's S.O.T. Teams will need even more determination than I needed on that cold night in February. Think of what it must have been like for Paul the apostle. How much determination did it take for Paul to get up after being stoned and left for dead? He had to go back into the very same city that had just stoned him. Acts 20 and 21 describes Paul's approach into Jerusalem where he knew he was heading for bonds and afflictions. Yet, he remained steadfast in his obedience to the Father. How much determination did it take for Jacob to wrestle with the Angel of the Lord? He did not give up, even after his hip had been dislocated, until he received his blessing. How much determination will it take when all the evil of the world comes against us and tries to kill us? Just think about how hard it is to stand firm in our commitment to the Lord when people around us make fun of us or persecute us for His name's sake. How hard is it to stand firm against the enemy when he tempts us with the things of the world? Christ's determination to obey the Father will be the same determination we will need in these last days.

Commitment and determination go hand in hand. Times are going to get extremely hard in the world for those believers who do not have a strong commitment and determination to follow the Lord. The Bible says in Matthew 24:24 that in the end times the enemy will try to deceive even the elect if it is possible. The enemy will be gunning for those believers who are operating in power under the anointing of the Holy Spirit.

We are going to have to put our faith in God, our eyes firmly fixed on Him, not wavering from our course for even a moment. We have been warned,

> "Because lawlessness is increased, most people's love will grow cold. But those who endure to the end, he will be save" (Matthew 24:12–13).

This means that it will not happen over night. People will slowly turn towards lawlessness and cultivate it in their hearts while justifying and protecting their sin much like protecting a small seedling as it matures into a full grown plant. This sin will ultimately choke out the love they had for the Lord. We must stay steadfast and determined in our love for Him. We must not allow our hearts to cultivate the seeds of sin. Isaiah describes it in this way:

> For you have forgotten the God of your salvation And have not remembered the rock of your refuge. Therefore you plant delightful plants And set them with vine slips of a strange god. In the day that you plant it you carefully fence it in, And in the morning you bring your seed to blossom; But the harvest will be a heap In a day of sickliness and incurable pain. (Isaiah 17:10–11)

If I had not made a continuous push during the swim out to the boats, the waves would have pushed me back towards the beach, and I would not have had enough strength to finish. If we deviate from our walk with God or take a break to pursue the things of the world, the enemy will swallow us up just like the waves.

The scripture clarifies the meaning of commitment when it says,

> "If a man makes a vow to the LORD, or takes an oath to bind himself with a binding obligation, he shall not violate his word; he shall do according to all that proceeds out of his mouth" (Numbers 30:2).

When we make a commitment we need to stick to it as if our life depends upon it. For God's S.O.T. Teams, it might just come to that. When our commitments are made in obedience to God's will then only God can release us from them. Our paths should not change unless we are receiving new orders from the Lord. When we are operating behind enemy lines, there is not much room for errors. The Lord will protect His servants, but if we waiver and step off course, we take our lives into our own hands.

When a SEAL learns how to patrol behind enemy lines, they are taught that the only truly safe place to step is in the footprint of the man in front of him. If we step anywhere else, we might be stepping on something that could blow our foot off! With Jesus walking as our point man, we can rest assure His footprints will lead us safely to our destination. We can be determined and resolved in our commitment to the Father when we know that our steps are aligned with His.

We are entrusted with extremely important missions in the SEALs because Commanding Officers know we are true to our word. When we say that we are going to do something then it is as good as done. God will grant missions of utmost importance to those who walk steadfastly in His ways. He will not entrust these kinds of tasks to someone He can not depend upon.

Peter learned this lesson the hard way. Jesus said, in regards to Peter,

> "I also say to you that you are Peter, and upon this rock I will build my church; and the gates of Hades will not overpower it" (Matthew 16:18).

Some might say, "But Peter denied the Lord three times." Yes, that is true. His denial is the price Peter paid to learn this lesson the hard way. At the end of his life he was so steadfast, committed, and determined that he was able to go through one of the worst deaths of all the disciples without wavering in his faith. He would not deny the Lord, so he was crucified on a cross like the Lord Jesus. Peter's cross, however, was placed upside down so that all the blood rushed to his head until he bled out the nose, eyes, and ears. Peter became that rock that would not be moved even when all of hell came against it.

Awhile ago, my mother received a word from the Lord about me by someone who was not aware of my military achievements. She was told I would be one who would rather die than surrender. No SEAL has ever been a prisoner of war because no SEAL has ever surrendered or been taken alive. Even though this is an underlying code in the SEAL teams, I believe He was referring to my spirit.

The Lord is glorified upon every martyr's death, but woe to the one that denies the Lord in the face of adversity. Jesus said in the book of Matthew,

> "But whoever denies me before men, I will also deny him before My Father Who is in heaven" (Matthew 10:33).

There is a difference between the servant who seeks to be a martyr and the servant who becomes a martyr because there is no other way. Like with everything in our walk with the Lord, we must seek His will and be obedient to His call. The Bible sheds some light on this subject in Revelations:

> And there was given to each of them a white robe; and they were told that they should rest for a little while longer, until the number of their fellow servants and their brethren who were to be killed even as they had been, would be completed also. (Revelations 6:11)

There is a set number established, and if the Lord has martyrdom in our future then we should stay steadfast, determined, and obedient. If He plans for us to be with Him some other way then we should not seek to be a martyr. I do not know one SEAL who wants to die in battle, but every SEAL I know would lay down his life for a fellow SEAL.

God is a determined God. He is looking for a determined people as the scripture says,

> "For the eyes of the Lord move to and fro throughout the earth that He may support those whose heart is completely His" (2 Chronicles 16:9).

His plans and purposes in the earth will come to pass. He is looking for someone to stand up and be accounted for. Like Isaiah I cry, "Here am I. Send me!"

We should not look behind, but as Paul says in Philippians, *"I press on toward the goal for the prize of the upward call of God in Christ Jesus" (Philippians 3:14).* If we keep our eyes on the Lord and His glory, we will not be able to see the darkness and evil that is all around us.

Chapter IV

Jack of all Trades and Masters of None

Many different phrases and motivational statements hang from the walls of the BUD/S training compound in Coronado, California, but there is one saying that best describes us as SEAL operators. We are called, "Jack of all trades and masters of none." It is not only a motto but a creed we live by in the SEAL teams. It means our skills allow us to do any job, but we do not master any one skill. This creed is evident in the acronym SEAL which stands for sea, air, and land. We can do any job, anywhere, and under any conditions. The motivation and desire to serve in a work environment requiring this "Jack of all trades" approach must come from within a candidate and is evidenced in their level of self motivation.

All of my life, I have wanted to be a part of whatever was going on around me. Growing up, I always had a problem trying to decide on what sport to play because I liked them all. Since I could not pick only one, I decided to participate in all of them. I had a desire to experience everything that life had to offer. One attractive aspect about being a SEAL is that we are always doing something different. We might be skydiving from twenty thousand feet in the morning, and later on that very same night we will be diving under some ship and placing explosives to the hull. Usually, missions involve the utilization of many different skills in order to accomplish it successfully. Do not get me wrong. I want to be the best that I can be in everything I do. I just like to do a lot of different things.

Most SEALs are the same way. If asked, most will confess to having participated in many different sports growing up, and they will probably admit to becoming easily bored with doing the same thing over and over. If they did not like variety in their lives, they would not be willing to pay the heavy price to become a Navy SEAL.

Being a "Jack of all trades and a master on none," requires an individual to have the special ability to adapt both physically and mentally to different situations. They must have the physical and mental ability to perform different skills and functions. In BUD/S, we must pass both physical and mental testing to show we have the capability to perform the duty. We must pass a rigorous physical examination to prove that our bodies can handle the requirements of the job. For example, a BUD/S candidate can not be color blind. The reasoning behind this restriction is that you must be able to differentiate between the colors blue, green, and red. Think back to a movie where the hero had to cut a certain colored wire to diffuse a bomb. Enough said. Also, when oxygen is breathed at depth it can become toxic to the human body, so we have to pass a diving physical to show that our bodies can handle the physiological stress of diving underwater on 100% oxygen rigs. Every human body handles oxygen consumption differently; therefore, it is important to ensure that the candidate's body will not react harshly to this highly oxygenated and pressurized environment. We must also pass an extensive psychological examination prior to BUD/S training. Many of these requirements that must be met cannot be learned, but must be given to us at birth.

There are many skills that can be learned, but they must be learned quickly. Being able to adapt to any situation helps speed up this learning process. SEALs must be able to learn new skills quickly because our training is so diverse it does not allow us the luxury of spending a lot of time on any one skill. Given enough time I can take just about anyone and teach them how to fire a weapon, scuba dive, or jump out of a plane. They might not be very proficient at it, but they will have learned enough to perform the action without killing themselves. SEALs must not only learn these skills in a short period of time, but they must be highly proficient at it also.

In BUD/S, we take a student that has never been scuba diving in his life, and in about eight weeks, they become extremely proficient divers. They must be able to dive regular compressed air as well as 100% oxygen rigs. Their skills must be performed during the day and at night. In order to pass their final dive, they must each be able to plan their dive using navigational skills, current charts, and dive physics. Their final dive is with a 100% oxygen rig. This dive will include transiting on the surface over four miles, submerge, and navigate using an underwater compass for over one mile. This must be accomplished without coming to the surface to look around. They must locate the target vessel docked amongst other vessels by using underwater navigational skills. They must be able to identify the correct ship while underwater, tag it, and dive to their extraction point, all without being detected by patrol ships that are constantly circling above them. This is just one example of a skill that must be learned quickly and must be used proficiently. They must perform every skill they learn in BUD/S in a similar fashion.

The ability to learn things quickly comes from God. It is a gift He has bestowed on these types of individuals. These are the types of individuals who seem to be good at everything they do. It is not because they are any better than anyone else. They just have a special gift God has given to them at birth.

This gift is also given to those who will serve in the S.O.T. Teams in God's Kingdom. They will be those individuals who give their lives to the Lord, and try to become involved in everything that is happening in the Church. They will not be satisfied with just praying for the sick. They will want to evangelize also. They will have a burning desire to help and shepherd others. They will want to teach or pastor. They will want to plant churches and go on the mission field. A prophetic gifting will run deep within them. They will be able to see themselves casting out demons and raising the dead. It will seem to those around them that they have lost their minds or are one of those extremists I talked about earlier. Truth be told, they have lost their minds, and they are extremists. They have lost their minds and taken on the mind of God. They will live extreme lives because of their desire to be obedient to the will of the Lord. These people will never seem to run out of energy. They are everywhere and doing everything. They are simply using the gift God has given them.

It is important that when we recognize this gift in these individuals, we do not try to stifle it. Actually, we will not be able to. I had many people tell me that I would never make a good SEAL, but that did not stop me from becoming one. Joseph fulfilled the dreams God gave him, even though his brothers sold him into slavery. This gift will drive a person to experience everything the Kingdom of God has to offer. Like I said before, God will get out of us what He has put into us. We are the only ones who can impede the will of God from working in our lives. God does not need anyone's permission to enlist us into His S.O.T. Team, except our own. We must say "yes" to the Lord, and we must be obedient to His calling. He will not force us to obey Him. His desire is for us to become willing subjects in our service to the King!

God's S.O.T. Team members will work as small units, sometimes even by themselves. Do not worry. God will always be by their side. He is the best swim buddy they could ever have. He will never become separated from us because of the storms and waves of the world. It says in Romans:

> For I am convinced that neither death, nor life, nor angels, nor principalities, nor things present, nor things to come, nor powers, nor height, nor depth, nor any other created thing, will be able to separate us from the love of God, which is in Christ Jesus our Lord. (Romans 8:38–39)

God's S.O.T. Teams will be gifted as apostles. They will have to be able to do anything the Lord needs them to do, at anytime, and in any condition. Like the apostle Paul, who was one of the first of his kind in the church, they will be prophesying, teaching, planting churches, casting out demons, healing the sick, and doing more for the Kingdom of God than I have time to write about. The gospel of John states that the world itself could not contain all of the books necessary to document everything

Jesus did while He walked the earth. It will be the same for these S.O.T. Team members.

Many of the skills needed to perform this duty will have been granted from the Father at birth. These are skills that can not be learned but are a special anointing from the Holy Spirit. It is not our own special abilities that will make this service possible but only by the grace of God in our lives. It is by understanding this truth that we will remain humble and contrite. SEALs, in and of themselves, are no different from anyone else. What sets them apart are the abilities they have to perform a specific task. If a SEAL lost his ability to walk, he could no longer serve as a Navy SEAL. I have seen SEALs get injured so badly they could no longer serve in the SEAL teams. If God were to remove the anointing from His S.O.T. Teams, they could no longer function in their specific role either.

On the other hand, some of the skills needed to perform this duty will have to be learned. The ability to learn these skills quickly will be vital to the mission of these S.O.T. Teams. In the SEAL Teams, a recent BUD/S graduate will spend, on average, about one to two years of intense training before they are considered ready for deployment. During that time, they must become proficient in every skill that a combat SEAL will need to be operational. The S.O.T. Teams in God's Kingdom will have to cope with this same predicament as well. As things heat up spiritually around the world, these operators are going to become needed more and more. Once they give their lives to the Lord, they will begin an intensive training regiment to prepare them to go into the battlefield. As Christ's return draws nearer, time will become a precious commodity and training will give way to "real world" spiritual combat operations.

In the SEAL Teams, we must learn new methods and techniques at the drop of a hat. We must be willing and capable to perform any function that might be required of us. We do not decide what missions we will go on either. We are given orders, and we perform our jobs with excellence every time. We are simply capable of performing this way every time we go out. God's S.O.T. Teams will have to respond in a similar fashion. They must be willing and capable to perform any function that is requested of them by the Lord or by the authorities placed over them. They will not get to pick their assignments but will perform whatever duties they are given with excellence and love in their hearts.

Evil in the world is intensifying right now at staggering rates. The governments of the world are identifying the need for an increase in Special Operation Units, like the SEALs. Likewise, the Church will need these members to step forward. Terrorism is just a physical manifestation of what is going on in the spirit. Special Operation Units will purify the world of terrorism. The S.O.T. Teams in the Church will usher in a move of the Holy Spirit that will purify the Bride of Christ. It will take people who are willing to pay a great price to be used by God to defeat this terrorist spirit. Things are going to become a lot worse before they become better. It is time for those who have been aching to serve in every role within the church to step up to the challenge!

Just think of the experiences and adventure that await us. We will be on the cutting edge of what God is doing. We will be used by God in ways that none of us can imagine. Jesus promised us that, *"all things are possible to him who believes" (Mark 9:23).* Lord, help me with my unbelief! I want to believe in every incredible possibility God brings my way. I am not exactly sure what God has in store for us, but there is one thing I am sure of. I want to be a part of it. God is calling for His "Jack of all trades and masters of none" to step up to the challenge and use the gifts God has given them.

Chapter V

Just Do It!

What does it mean to be spontaneous? Do we take forever to decide on what we are going to wear, or do we throw caution to the wind and put on whatever we come across first? I have found that for most of my life, I have been the latter. It has been both a curse and a blessing. I have had to "pull my foot out of my mouth" for saying the first thing that came into my head, but I have also made some of the best decisions in my life because I did not "beat around the bush". Through proper training and gainful experience, the gift of spontaneity can be used to allow maximum efficiency in the decision making process.

Back in 1990, I found myself in college with no real plans for my life. I was competing on a NCAA Division I cross-country team when an injury side lined me. I was not serving the Lord at the time, so I tried to escape reality by making a career out of drinking in the local taverns. Approaching it like everything else I do in life, I tackled it with a vengeance. Pretty soon I was broke, my grades had fallen, and I knew I was in trouble.

One day, as I was drinking myself into a stupor, I decided I had to make a change. My parents have been in the ministry for as long as I can remember, but I did not want anything to do with their lifestyle or with God. I did know I wanted out of town, and I knew I needed to do something that would give me a decent living, so I decided to join the military. The next day I was in my car driving towards the recruiting offices near my home in Conroe, Texas. As I drove into the parking lot, I looked around at the different branches of the military. One sign said Army, one Navy, one Marines, and one Air Force. I sat in my car for about one minute while trying to decide which one to go into. That was about all it took for me to decide on the Navy. After all, I thought to myself, I like the ocean, and I just felt a gut instinct that said it was the right choice.

In His mercy, God will sometimes allow outside circumstances to lead us even if we are not listening to Him. Like Jonah, He was going to steer me down a path that would eventually lead me to repentance. I thought I could run away from God if I could just get away from everything and everyone who reminded me of Him. I tried to ignore the simple fact that God is everywhere.

As I walked through the door, the recruiter met me. I did not want to waste time, so I let him know right away that I was ready to join and leave the very same day. I just wanted him to sign me up. He told me that I had to take a placement test first, which I did. I scored very well on it, so he wanted to show me some advanced technical jobs they had to offer. I told him I was not interested because I had just dropped out of college, and the last thing I wanted to do was sit in a classroom all day. He asked me what I felt like doing. I looked around the office and saw a poster of some guys who were scuba diving, jumping out of planes, and carrying weapons. It was 1990 and the first Gulf War had not been fought yet. Hollywood and the news media had not yet had the opportunity to sell us to the world, so I did not know what I was getting myself into when I pointed to the sign and said, "I want to do that!" My mind had been made up, and I knew what I would be doing with the rest of my life, but the story does not end there.

I gave my life to the Lord seven years later, and after having served ten years in the military, I decided to get out. There was, however, one major difference between how I had decided to join, and how I had decided to end my service. I joined for my own selfish reasons, but I ended my career because I felt it was what the Lord wanted me to do. Either way, they both happened very quickly for me.

Since that time, I have made a few more snap decisions significantly altering my life and the lives of my wife and children. These quick decisions were not rash decisions but were based upon my desire to be obedient to the voice of the Father. Sometimes, it is a still small voice, and sometimes, I feel a strong urge or almost a compulsion. Usually, however, these feelings come on quickly, and if I do not act quickly, they will pass. The Lord will not leave the door open forever.

When the children of Israel reached the Jordon, they were told by God to cross over, but they refused. He did not tell them to take their time to think about it. Instead, He told them the door had closed, and it would not reopen again until they were all dead. Only their children and the two obedient spies, Joshua and Caleb, would be allowed to enter when the door reopened.

Navy SEALs must be able to make decisions quickly and correctly. They must use gut instinct, analytical thinking, problem solving, and past experiences to come to a decision that will best suit the given situation. The key is that it is quick, and they do not second guess themselves. One consequence for making a bad decision in the SEALs is death to ourselves or those around us. Usually, the more confident a SEAL is in himself, his team, and his equipment, the better decisions he will make. If there is any doubt then it will cause a delay in his decision making abilities.

During the time that I worked as a SEAL recruiter, I would tell possible candidates that if I had to talk them into the program then someone else, including themselves, would be able to talk them out of it. I would tell them everything about the program, and then I would usually give them until the next day to decide. Everyone I put into the program who made it through had made up their mind to join within twenty-four hours of speaking with me. Sometimes, like in my case, it happened right there in the office. If they were able to quickly make the decision to join, using only essential information and a strong gut instinct, they would stand a better chance of holding firm to that decision no matter what anyone said to them and no matter what suffering they might go through. Why? Their self determination and drive would have been birthed from a decisive decision that was based on their own instinct rather than my persuasive speech. The same can be said about committing our lives to the Lord.

The process of dedicating our lives to the Lord must include the conviction of our sins. We must feel it deep within us for there to be a true conversion. If we only give our lives to the Lord because someone else persuaded us to believe it would be the best "business" decision with the most benefits then our commitment will never last. We will change our mind as soon as someone else offers us a choice that we believe has better benefits. There are those within the Body of Christ today who have joined for some reason other than for the fact that they are sinners who need the blood of Jesus to restore their relationship to the Father. The message of the cross has become lost in many of the churches in America today. We must have felt a conviction of our sin and made our decision based upon the fact that we are sinners, and our only hope lies in Jesus. If we feel this conviction in our spirit then our decision becomes one of necessity and not convenience. A SEAL candidate has a better chance when they join the program because they believe that being a SEAL is what they were meant to be. They feel like they need to be there. Those who must be persuaded to join are less likely to graduate because when the going gets rough, they will be looking to trade in their new lifestyle for one that has less suffering. It will not take a great salesman to persuade them either.

I like everything about being a SEAL, but if I had to pick the aspect I like the least, it would be jumping out of perfectly good airplanes. I have always had a fear of heights. It was not the fall that scared me but the landing. I use to have nightmares as a child of falling off a cliff and into space. I would never land but just keep falling with this impending doom that I would soon land . . . violently! I would usually wake up all sweaty and scared to death! This was something I had to overcome when I went through free-fall school. It was like reliving my childhood nightmares, only this time it was for real.

When I was learning to skydive, I had to first practice everything with my feet firmly planted on the ground. I had to learn how to position my body in the air, so I could fall in a stable position. Otherwise, I would spin out of control, and when I tried to deploy my parachute it would roll up, not open, and I would find myself crashing headlong into the earth at about 120 M.P.H. I also had to practice emergency procedures in the event that my parachute did not open or something else happened out of the ordinary. Before I boarded the plane and during the flight to my drop zone, I would go over everything that could happen during the jump, and exactly what I would do if something went wrong. It was during one of these jumps that I had the opportunity to use the emergency procedures I had learned.

We were jumping from about twelve thousand feet which roughly allows for about two to three minutes of free fall time before we have to pull our rip cord to deploy our parachute. This amount of time depends, of course, on the altitude that we are set to pull at. On this particular jump, I believe we were pulling at two thousand feet. As I approached the deployment altitude, I checked to make sure no other jumpers were above me, and I began to go through my pull sequence. I pulled my rip cord and quickly realized my parachute did not come off my back. This abnormality is known as a "bag lock." Without thinking and without any hesitation, I went into my emergency procedures. As I went through the procedures, I did not think about what I was doing. My body and mind were on autopilot. All the practicing I had done with my feet on the ground had seared the movements into my mind, and now it had taken over. The procedures worked well, and the parachute opened above me. I had the ability to make rapid decisions because I had confidence in myself, the procedures, and my equipment. I did not need to second guess what I was doing because I knew the procedures would work. If I had started second guessing myself, I would have panicked, ran out of time, and been planted into the field below me, along with whatever crops were growing there at the time.

When the Angel of the Lord approached Joseph in a dream, He told him to take the baby Jesus and Mary, and move to Egypt. Joseph did not delay. Because of his quick decision to obey, he was able to protect Jesus from King Herod, who was seeking to kill Him.

God has chosen to use dreams as a way of communicating with me as well over the years. He has used dreams to give me insights into the things of the Spirit. I have had many dreams where I was put into a situation that required me to act quickly or many lives would be lost, including my own. On one particular evening, I had a dream where I was standing next to a concrete wall. Off in the distance a mushroom cloud appeared, but no one noticed it expect for me. I shouted to those around me to follow me as I stepped behind a concrete wall. Those who heard my voice and obeyed were spared as seconds later a nuclear blast went by vaporizing everyone and everything in its path. The only survivors were those who stood with me behind the concrete wall. In another dream, I was on an island, and I was standing on the beach. I felt the Lord tell me to move to higher ground. I shouted to those around me to follow me, and I went to the top of a mountain. It was the highest place on the island. When I got to the top, I turned around to see a great wave swallow up the island. I watched as those who did not follow me were drowned by the violence of the monstrous wave. The wave covered the entire island except for the tops of the mountains. Those who came with me lived, and those who did not, died. I believe the Lord has shown me how He has plans to use me someday to forewarn others of coming calamities, so they might be spared.

I believe in a similar way, a prophetic gifting, or

having an uncanny ability to hear from the Lord, will help these S.O.T. Teams operate in a way that will preserve the lives of many members within the Church. Even unbelievers will benefit from these individuals, should they choose to listen to them. Remember Rahab from the city of Jericho? She was a citizen of Jericho and therefore an enemy of God, but because she decided to listen to the two spies and help them, her life and the lives of her family were spared. God is merciful, and He wishes that none should perish either in this life or the next. He will hold off His hand of judgment for as long as possible, but even when He must act as the Righteous Judge that He is, He will give prior warning to those who will listen.

There will be many events happening in the days to come that will require quick and decisive decision making in order to survive. When the Lord says move, we will not have the time to pack up our belongings. It says in Matthew:

> Therefore when you see the ABOMINATION OF DESOLATION which was spoken of through Daniel the prophet, standing in the holy place (let the reader understand), then those who are in Judea must flee to the mountains. Whoever is on the housetop must not go down to get the things out that are in his house. Whoever is in the field must not turn back to get his cloak. But woe to those who are pregnant and to those who are nursing babies in those days! But pray that your flight will not be in the winter, or on a Sabbath. For then there will be a great tribulation, such as has not occurred since the beginning of the world until now, nor ever will. Unless those days had been cut short, no life would have been saved; but for the sake of the elect those days will be cut short. (Matthew 24:15–22)

Even though this scripture applies to a specific event, I believe our decisions in these end days will need to be guided by the Holy Spirit; so we can make timely maneuvers in order to avoid the judgments that will be coming to the earth. We can already see events unfolding in nature where lives could have been spared had the world been warned and had they listened to the warnings. The time for procrastination is quickly coming to an end in the Church.

The ability to hear from the Lord and make decisive decisions will not only spare us from coming judgments to the earth but will also allow us an opportunity to be used as the Lord moves in His Spirit to save the lost. We need to be in the right place, at the right time, and doing the right thing, if we want to be used in the coming revival to our nation and the world.

One of the jobs of a SEAL is to rescue hostages. Satan has taken many hostages since the fall of mankind, and now it is time for us to take them back! When the Lord sends His revival He will need people to move quickly to gather in and direct those who will be flooding our churches. It will be vital that we are hearing clearly from the Lord, so that none will be stolen back by the enemy.

We will have to do exactly as the Holy Spirit instructs us, and do it quickly. In the military, we are taught to obey orders immediately. The reason is not to take away our ability to think for ourselves but to teach us there might be times requiring our absolute obedience to save our lives or the lives of those around us. In the heat of battle, many things are going on. We are not always privy to all the information that is being put out at the time. If my officer tells me to move, it is probably for a good reason. I must have faith in his abilities as my leader.

It is our faith in the Lord that will enable us to make these rapid decisions needed in these end times. I believe God's S.O.T. Teams will be given great faith from the Father. Faith is not something we can just make happen. It is a gift from the Lord. The more we use it the more He will give us. Sometimes, He gives us the faith needed for a particular event in our lives. There have been times when I have really believed God was going to heal someone, and after I prayed for them, they were healed. There have also been times when I have really felt strongly that God was telling me to give a word from Him to a complete stranger, and when I gave them the word the person validated my feelings. Then there are those times that I have wanted to believe God would heal someone, but I just could not seem to muster the faith that was needed, and when I prayed for them nothing seemed to happen. This can happen when the grace is not there. I lacked the faith, they did, or we both did. There could be many different reasons why this might happen, but I am convinced the faith comes from God, not from our own desires to believe.

The book of Acts gives a report on this faith when it states,

> "When they had arrived and gathered the church together, they began to report all things that God had done with them and how He had opened a door of faith to the Gentiles" (Acts 14:27).

It is this open door of faith that I ask the Lord to give to His Church. If the desire alone for this kind of faith were enough, I believe we would already see the kind of miracles happening in the world today that Jesus told us to expect. The Lord in His infinite wisdom has not released it on the earth yet, but it is coming.

The Lord's S.O.T. Teams will operate in this great level of faith. Except for the Son of God, I do not believe any man yet has walked in the kind of faith we will experience when the Lord opens the door. Remember what Jesus said about us? He said:

> Truly, truly, I say to you, he who believes in Me, the works that I do, he will do also; and greater works than these he will do; because I go to the Father. Whatever you ask in My name, that will I do, so that the Father may be glorified in the Son. (John 14:12–13)

He said we would do greater things than He did while He walked the earth. Lord let it be! Imagine what it will be like. Remember in Acts 5:14–16 when Peter's shadow healed the sick as he walked by? I can see entire hospitals emptied out. They will become empty because the sick are being healed simply because someone obeys the voice of the Lord and walks down the hallways declaring their healing. Imagine entire psychiatric hospitals freed because the demons that were terrorizing those souls fled at the sight of Jesus walking towards them. Not our King in the flesh but the Spirit of Jesus, who will shine out of those who live perfectly obedient lives, abandoned to His call.

The time for decisive decision making has come. This gift is given to us by our Father, and it must be used in our quest to live in absolute obedience to Him. We have to be like Christ. How did He live His life? He tells us in John 10 when He says,

> "Do you not believe that I am in the Father, and the Father is in Me? The words that I say to you I do not speak on My own initiative, but the Father abiding in Me does His works" (John 10:10)

This kind of obedience will be guided by faith, and this faith will be based on our love for the Father and His children. Our decision making will be based upon His will, and His will is based upon love. Throughout history, God has proven Himself as a Father Who is quick to love, and so must we be.

The following four chapters identify character traits that must be utilized by both the U.S. military's Special Operation Units and God's Special Operation Teams. These can be taught and learned if they are not already utilized in their lives.

Chapter VI

The Quiet Professional

Every year about a thousand or so young men show up to BUD/S, and all of them have their own reasons for being there. A few might want to see if they are up to the challenge, and a few more might want to accomplish something that few men have ever achieved. There are even those who sign up, simply because they think it would be "cool," and it would give them an identity that would demand respect. When I was recruiting, I remember one young man telling me he wanted to become a Navy SEAL, so he could kill people legally. Needless to say, I kindly asked him to leave my office wondering all the while which lucky recruiter from the other services had this guy coming his way. What did all of these people have in common? They all wanted something for themselves.

I myself had similar motives when I walked into that Navy office in Conroe, Texas about fifteen years ago. I grew up as a skinny kid, always feeling I had to defend myself against the bullies of the world. Many would say I had a fairly large chip on my shoulders. Of course, at 5' 10" and 135 pounds, any chip would have been large. Like I said before, I had just dropped out of college, had no real place to be, and so I decided to travel the world and leave behind the little town I had grown to despise. When I went into the Navy recruitment office, I knew I was not leaving without a job. This was before the media had come out with all the SEAL movies and documentaries, so I had no idea what a Navy SEAL was. I later found out my recruiter did not know much about it either. When I told him I wanted to be a Navy SEAL, he looked at me, and a big grin began to form on his face. I could see him looking me over, and then he said, "Are you sure you don't want to do something else? You would never make it. Navy SEALs are a lot bigger than you and hardly anybody makes it through the training anyways." The chip on my shoulder grew twice its size that day, and I knew there was no going back. I told him if he did not give me a chance I was joining another service. "Alright, alright" he said, "but don't say I didn't warn you." I later had an opportunity to go back to the recruiting station in Conroe, Texas and visit my recruiter to let him know he was right. Hardly anybody does make it through the training. I truly thanked him for helping me join, and then I left. Why did I not strut around, rub in the fact that he was wrong, and clearly express the fact that I had made it despite his opinions of me? I had joined because I was told I could not make it, because it was too hard, and because I was not "cut out" for it. It was my pride urging me to join, but something else had gotten me through the training.

Every candidate learns there is one reason to become a Navy SEAL. We do it for the love of the job. We have to love the job for what it is, and not what we might think it could be for us. It has to become a part of us. The members we serve with are our brothers. All the glory we gain from our service goes to the SEAL community. Our identity is there, in the community, and in the team.

Humility is the key word. I went to the training bolstered by pride, but I soon learned humility was the key to getting me out alive and in one piece. I know most people probably do not consider SEALs as being a humble group of individuals, and in a way, they would be correct. We are humbled in our knowledge that we are part of a team that relies upon each other to get a job done. No one SEAL is the greatest, but together there is no job too big and no challenge to daunting. When we are successful in a mission the team earns the glory. We understand there is a job to do, and so we do it. If any glory or fame is sought, it is from those we serve with and not from the outside community.

The public has an almost mythological concept about the Navy SEALs. While this helps us by giving us the ability to intimidate our enemies, it can harm us if we allow ourselves to become prideful. Pride will lead to over-confidence, and over-confidence will lead to failure.

In the past ten years, there has been a lot of information released to the public about the SEAL Teams through the media, but the Special Warfare Community has not allows been so liberal in supplying information to the media and the press. Secrecy has been a cornerstone of Special Warfare from its conception. We use the element of surprise to pull off some amazing feats. When a candidate enters the training it is made perfectly clear to him that many of the things he will do will never be heard of by the general public. Sometimes, even our own family members will never know of them. Awards and recognition might only be awarded after a mission has become unclassified years later, if ever. Or, they are written up in an obscure way so as to keep the exact facts of the mission a secret. Everything we do is not so "cloak and dagger," and there are many times we are rewarded for a job well done, but SEALs are not usually in it for the medal count.

I remember one time being chosen to perform a mission with a very high security clearance rating. We were not even told the exact details of the mission until we arrived to the site where we were going. We were just told what type of equipment to bring and approximately how long we would be gone for. Our mission was to test some new high tech equipment being developed for the Special Warfare Community. We were sent to an isolated island to test the equipment, so that information of our testing would not leak out. The equipment was extremely expensive and very high tech. Early into the testing a key component needed for the test broke. There was no way to fix the equipment in our remote environment, and it would take weeks to get another one to the site. We were going to have to scrub the mission, losing valuable time and money. All of a sudden, I had an idea. I was able to develop a system allowing us to continue the testing using some modified equipment we had brought. The mission was a success, and because of the importance of the mission, I was put in for a medal. When the award document was written, it mentioned nothing of the secret mission. Instead, all it said was that I was being awarded a medal for my ingenuity and dedication to service. There was a general statement about how I set up a temporary system enabling a training mission to be accomplished. Did I mind if all of the facts did not come out? No. To tell the truth, I did not even want the medal. I had received the admiration of my fellow SEALs who were there during the testing, and that was enough. The people who were there from outside agencies were amazed that we were able to pull it off, and our actions brought glory to the SEAL community. That is what it is all about.

When a SEAL candidate goes through BUD/S and even after they become a full fledged SEAL, they go through many times of suffering. BUD/S purposely causes suffering in order to make candidates look within themselves to see if they really want this lifestyle. Being a SEAL is just that, a lifestyle. The lessons you learn are taken into all aspects of your life. The suffering is then worn as a badge of honor for those who stay in the program. The badge is not worn externally but internally. It is a badge only another SEAL can identify and empathize with. There is no glory in the suffering for the one who suffers. The glory is for the ideal we are suffering for. It is a way to show the SEAL community that we are a part of the whole, and we are willing to pay any price to bear witness to that fact. If someone suffers alone, for some reason of their own, and with no one to witness the suffering, what glory does it bring? If they suffer for someone else or for some cause and there are witnesses, the glory goes to the cause or to the one the suffering is for.

I remember when I first gave my life to the Lord, and I began to feel unrest in my spirit. I wanted to do more for the Lord than I was doing at the time. I wanted to aspire to a higher calling. I remember telling people how it was truly possible to live in perfect obedience to the Father just as Christ did. We should be raising the dead, healing people, and casting out demons! We should be hearing the voice of the Father clearly and acting on His every whisper. Most people listened to me with reservation. Many people want to believe it is possible to live in perfect obedience, but most believe it is not probable. I believe it is not only possible but probable. Actually, it is how God wants us to live.

What I did not know at the time was that I was being motivated to live for Christ in this way for the same reason I had joined the Navy. People told me it was crazy, and I would not be able to do it. Just like my recruiter, they were partially right. I could never live this way with pride being my motivation. I had to learn the same lesson I learned in BUD/S. If I wanted to be like Christ, living in perfect obedience to the Father, I would have to learn to be motivated by my love for Him. I would have to learn to love Him for Who He was, and not what He could do for me. I would have to desire His ideals beyond everything else. Many people will have their own reasons for wanting to aspire to this higher calling, but there can be no reason other than our love for Him. There can not be anything in it for us as individuals, but everything must be for the Lord and His Kingdom. Just like in the SEALs, we can join for the wrong reason as long as we can identify the right reason and be willing to accept it. If not, we will "wash out" of the program, guaranteed.

In the SEAL teams, I experienced much suffering. Likewise, in our service to the Lord, there will be much suffering. It is promised to us in the Word. Remember the words of Jesus when He says:

> If you were of the world, the world would love its own; but because you are not of the world, but I chose you out of the world, because of this the world hates you Remember the word that I said to you, 'A slave is not greater than his master' If they persecuted Me, they will also persecute you; if they kept My word, they will keep yours also. But all these things they

> will do to you for My name's sake, because they do not know the One who sent Me. (John 15:19–21)

The higher someone climbs within the rank structure of the U.S. military (i.e. Admiral, Commander-in-Chief, etc.) or the more sensitive their job position (i.e. Special Operations, intelligence, etc.), the more the enemies of the U.S. would like to see them removed, or better yet, captured. This is because they pose a greater threat.

There was a Navy SEAL during the Vietnam War who won the Medal of Honor for performing a vital rescue mission behind enemy lines. His mission was to rescue a downed pilot who was also a high ranking officer within the U.S. military. The SEAL's name was Tommy Norris. He dressed up as a Vietnamese fisherman and went up river with a South Vietnamese soldier in a small fishing vessel, far behind enemy lines. He rescued the officer and brought him out safely. The reason the mission was so vital was because the officer was very high ranking, and he had a lot of very sensitive intelligence stored within his brain. The enemy was doing everything they could to find him. The U.S. military did not want the enemy to get their hands on this downed pilot because capture would lead to torture and torture could lead to divulged secrets. If the enemy was able to get the sensitive information from the downed pilot, it could lead to the deaths of many more military personnel.

The enemy knows if God's S.O.T. Teams are successful, the Body of Christ will enter into the final stages of preparation for the return of Christ. Imagine what damage could be done to the Body of Christ if someone who is working closely with the Lord allows pride to turn them from Him, and captured by the enemy, they begin working against the Church instead of for it. The Lord will have His Son's Bride ready for His return, but His return can be delayed because of the Church's refusal to participate. It is because of His great love that He gives us the choice to obey Him or not. He wanted the children of Israel to enter the Promised Land, but because of their refusal, that entry was delayed. Why did they refuse to enter? They refused because the intelligence gatherers gave them a bad report and caused fear to enter their midst. Jesus will return and bring His kingdom, but the enemy knows they can cause damage to the Body of Christ and delay His coming. It is for this reason they fight so venomously to delay His return for as long as possible. Pride will ruthlessly attack these forerunners of the Lord in an attempt to cause dissention amongst the ranks, decreasing the efficiency with which these S.O.T. Team members will operate.

The S.O.T. Teams will be targeted by the enemies of God. Our enemies would gladly take the life of any believer, but they would consider believers like Paul the Apostle as trophies in their war against God. They would try to use these trophies to inflict pain upon the Body of Christ and the heart of God. This attack on the S.O.T. Teams will be intense, but they will have a special cloak of humility given to them by God to help them not only endure the attacks but flourish in them. They will take the plans of the enemy and use it against them. Instead of allowing the enemy to use them as fallen trophies, they will bring great glory to the Lord through their suffering for the Kingdom, and they will inspire those in the Body of Christ to take on the cloak of humility in their own lives. We have a saying in the SEAL Teams for when it becomes cold, dark, wet, and miserable outside. We announce, "Looks like good operating weather!" Those kinds of conditions give us an opportunity to shine by going where others fear to tread.

Just like in the SEAL teams, God's S.O.T. Teams will face severe consequences for falling to the temptations of pride. Failure in the SEAL Teams could easily lead to death. God's S.O.T. Teams will be held to an extremely high standard because of their great anointing and surplus of gifts. Jesus said in Luke, *"From everyone who has been given much, much will be required" (Luke 17:48).* Failure to live at this high standard for the S.O.T. Teams could have dire consequences. Look at what happened to Sampson because of his pride. He allowed the Philistines to cut off his hair, thereby breaking his vow unto the Lord. Maybe he just thought he was too witty for them, or maybe, he began to believe the strength came from within himself and not from God. I for one do not want to experience the consequences for allowing my pride to get in the way while working under this special anointing of the Holy Spirit.

Fresh graduates of the SEAL program usually look upon the more veteran SEALs with respect and honor. They try to emulate them in their operational prowess. As a disciple of Christ we should look to Christ as our example and for our inspiration. With this in mind, the one time Jesus described Himself in the scripture He says, *"For I am gentle and humble in heart" (Matthew 11:29).* Humility is one of the keys to walking in the power of the Holy Spirit.

The more important and sensitive a mission is, the more proven a SEAL must be. In Numbers 12:3, Moses is described as *"very humble, more than any man who was on the face of the earth,"* but God trained him in the desert for forty years before He sent him on his mission to deliver the children of Israel. He knew Moses had to understand humility before He could let him serve as the mouth piece of God. He took a prince and made him a sheep herder. The reason for this training in humility becomes more evident when we see his punishment for his disobedience in Kadesh. Because of his disobedience he was not allowed to enter into the Promised Land. I believe it was his pride that caused Moses to disobey the Lord when he struck the rock instead of just speaking to it. He had gotten angry at the children of Israel because of their constant complaining. If Moses, the most humble man on the face of the earth, could stumble because of pride then how much more should we guard against it?

Humility is a character trait seen in all of the great men of God throughout history. In the SEAL Teams we wear camouflage and face paint to help hide us from the enemy. When a SEAL platoon is dressed up in battle array it is hard to tell the difference between them. They all look alike. During Vietnam, the enemy simply called them "the men with green faces." Humility will be the S.O.T. Team's camouflage. It will be a special cloak worn by God's S.O.T. Teams to hide them from the enemy as they work behind the enemy's lines, and it will make those who wear it indistinguishable one from another.

Chapter VII

Yes Sir!

When it comes to morals and virtue, society has been in a constant state of degeneration. Sin is everywhere, and if you want to see where we are heading as a nation just look to our youth. I have had the opportunity to spend three years recruiting for the Navy and the Special Warfare Community, looking largely to the young people of this nation to fill the roles needed in the U.S. military. I must say, it saddens my heart to think of where our nation was 200 years ago compared to where we are right now. I am not saying that there are not those who truly love the Lord, but in general, our society has done a great disservice to our youth by making decisions for them like taking the Lord out of our schools. We have made great strides as a nation in the areas of science and technologies, but our nation's moral values have experienced a crash worse than any crash Wall Street has ever seen.

There are many reasons for our moral downfall as a

society, but I believe there is an underlying reason that has allowed this decline to occur so rapidly. There is a deep seed of rebellion in this nation. Ironically, this rebellion began as a determination in the hearts of a people who wanted to be free to worship God in their own way. This desire has slowly turned into a selfish desire to be free to pursue our own personal dreams and ambitions. To be free to follow God is a wonderful thing, but being free to follow our own heart's desires leads us down a path that Satan has used many times before to lead God's children away from Him.

In the beginning, Satan rebelled against God because of his own selfish desires to be greater than his Creator. Adam and Eve also rebelled against God because of their selfish desires to be like God. Today people rebel because they want to be their own god, so they can determine their own future.

When someone joins the military, the first thing they must do is go to boot camp. It is there that they are stripped of their individuality, and they are developed into team players. They are taught obedience by placing them into a structured environment, giving them rules to follow, and disciplining them if they break those rules. We teach them there are consequences for the actions they take and show them that obeying their authorities is a good thing. They learn what a chain of command is, and we show them where they fall into that chain. We show them the entire chain of command from the Commander in Chief, our president; to the lowest level, themselves. We teach them the importance of obedience and how the consequences of disobedience could be death, theirs and their teammates. Usually, when someone graduates from boot camp the people that knew them before can hardly recognize them. Not because they look so different, but because they carry themselves differently and behave like a different person.

In today's society we judge disobedience on a sliding scale. For example, speeding down the freeway 10 M.P.H. over the speed limit is considered acceptable behavior by most. Yeah, but no one is really getting hurt, right? How about cheating on our taxes, jaywalking, or running a stop sign? How about taking a pen from work that does not belong to us? What would happen if I told a coworker that taking a pen from work without asking is stealing, and stealing is against the law? They would probably laugh me out of the office. The truth is that all of these actions are acts of disobedience. Disobedience that might seem trivial to us today is only trivial because our society has judged the action on this sliding scale. Most people would not ever consider murdering someone because the act of murder is just too evil, but most people do not mind speeding because nobody is really getting hurt by it.

In the SEAL teams, we do not even address the issue of disobedience because it is common sense that when we are given an order, we obey it. We do not have to worry about an order being disobeyed, so we give a lot of latitude in how orders are followed. I might tell someone under me to prepare the equipment for a dive. I am not going to give them specific orders on how to do it because I know they will handle it in the way they were trained. I do not have to micromanage those under me because I know it will be done the way I want it done. I do not expect my men to break the rules because they have all been trained to abide by them and to work within the system. Of course, there are the rare exceptions when someone breaks a rule, but they are quickly and sternly disciplined. I can not remember anytime though, that a SEAL disobeyed a direct order. It just does not happen.

The reason obedience is so important in the SEAL Teams is that we are working in a very dangerous environment. Many times if things are not done in a specific way and in a specific order, men might die. By questioning an order from a superior officer I am saying I have a better way to do something, or my ideas are better than his ideas. How can I come to that conclusion when I do not know all of the facts? When we are working in a team environment, someone has to be in charge. Everyone has his own tasks to take care of, and with all of these different things going on at once it would be impossible for me to know what everyone else is doing. That is what the leader is for. It is his job to know what everyone is doing, so he can coordinate everyone's individual efforts into one effort. He takes in all of the information and tells us what to do to make the mission a success. He is taking in my input and combining it with the input of others in order to see the whole picture. Since he has the whole picture, he can determine that I need to make some small change immediately to avoid some problem ahead. If he sees this and orders me to make the change, I must trust in his decision and do it with no questions asked. Granted, our daily lives might not have the same dangers as I have faced in the SEAL Teams, but the rule still applies.

What we must realize is that we chose to be put under this person's authority. Everyone in the military made the decision to enlist, so they chose to put themselves in the position to have to obey orders given to them from their superiors. By choosing to live in the United States, we have chosen to have the authorities of this country over us; therefore, we must obey them even if we do not totally agree with them. It says in Romans,

> "Every person is to be in subjection to the governing authorities for there is no authority except from God, and those which exist are established by God" (Romans 13:1).

"What if I am told to do something by my boss that is illegal?" Good question. When I was in the military, we had something called the Uniform Code of Military Justice. This document outlined the laws that every service member had to abide by. Not only did we have to abide by this document, but we also had to abide by all Federal and State laws as well. The military is held to a higher standard than the general public. If I was given an order I did not agree with, I had to obey the order. If it was the wrong decision then the person who gave me the order would have to answer for it, not me. If I was given an order that went against the Uniform Code of Military Justice, Federal, or State laws, in other words an unlawful order, I could refuse to obey the order based upon its conflict with the law. But I had better be absolutely sure I was correct in my judgment of the law because I would have to answer for my actions. The same thing would apply to all authority in all walks of life.

The same rule applies to the Church as well. When someone gives their life to the Lord, they are allowing themselves to be placed into a chain of command in the Kingdom of God. "But," we say, "the Church is a family, not the military." Well, let us approach it from that angle for a moment. Families have fathers and mothers, right? We must all realize and acknowledge that authority will always be in our lives. The Kingdom of God is no exception. I believe it operates more closely to the military than it does to family life anyways. Families tend to operate more closely to democracies where everyone has the ability to voice their own opinion, but the parents end up making the final decision. The military is operated more closely to a monarchy than a democracy. Jesus is our King and that constitutes a monarchy. In a monarchy, the king makes the law and everyone obeys it no matter what the law is. If we want to live in the kingdom we must be willing to do whatever the king says. If we do not want to obey the law then we would be better off leaving the kingdom with our head still on our shoulders. The Church is not a democracy. We do not vote on what we think we should do or what laws should apply to us. We have a King, and He has already decreed His laws for His kingdom.

When Jesus returns, He will bring His kingdom along with Him. Until this happens, He has placed members of His Church in leadership roles to oversea the operations here on earth. They are known as pastors and apostles. When we decide to join a congregation, we are professing our willingness to have the pastor lead us. If the pastor wants the leadership team in the church to wear a certain style of clothing then the leadership team should be dressed in the appropriate manner. I was ordered to wear uniforms while I was in the Navy. Even though I did not always like the uniform, I had to wear it. I was even told exactly how I was to wear it. Imagine if the pastor told the leadership team to make sure their shoes were highly polished, and if they failed his inspection they would have to polish them again and again until they got it right! This might sound extreme, but only because we are so use to doing our own thing and worrying about our own ambitions. Did the Levite priests in the Old Testament complain about the clothing they were ordered to wear?

What about something affecting us all, like the style of worship music being played in our congregations every Sunday morning? Should we have a say in what kind of music gets played? Should we pass around a hat and have everyone put their own opinion in it? When I served in the Navy, what would have happened to me if I stood before my Commanding Officer's desk and told him I did not like the way he handled the awards ceremonies? What if I told him I thought we should all get to participate in the decision making process for all future ceremonial rituals? I would quickly learn that there is only one person in charge, and that it was not me. If I did not want to obey the orders of those put over me, I could always leave the SEAL Teams and go back into the regular Navy, even though I would run into the same problems there.

Should those members within the Body of Christ, who do not want to obey their leadership, leave their congregation and go elsewhere in search of a church where they will be willing to submit and be obedient? They may if they choose to, but I give them fair warning. If someone leaves a congregation because of their unwillingness to obey, they will find that they will have the same problem everywhere else they go as well. If they have a problem with obedience or their desire to obey, they should question why they gave their lives to the Lord in the first place; or if in fact, they ever did at all. It is true that we can all hear from God ourselves. I can also see what is happening around me when I am on a SEAL mission. This does not mean I can disobey a lawful order from my commander. If the pastor gives us a lawful order then we should, no, must, obey it. Individuals who leave a church because of their unwillingness to submit are seeking to find someone to lead them who will not demand of them what they are not willing to freely give. Guess what! The Bible says that when we give our lives to the Lord we are no longer to live our lives by our own will; instead, we are to live every moment of our lives according to His will and His will alone. According to His word, His will is for us to submit to those He has placed over us.

How can we tell what is a lawful or unlawful order from our leaders in the Church? We have a Uniform Code of Military Justice in the Church as well. It is called the Bible. In this document, it tells us all the laws we are to obey as followers of Christ. If my pastor gives me an unlawful order, I must choose to either stand on the Word of God and decline or follow the unlawful order. If I decline his orders, the pastor will be the only one having to answer to the Lord for his actions, but if he is giving me an unlawful order I might want to think about finding a congregation where the pastor obeys the Word of God. If I choose to follow the unlawful order then I will also be held accountable. I had better be sure that the order is unlawful though because if I disobey a lawful order, I alone will be held accountable. A lawful order is any order given to me by a superior that does not contradict the Uniform Code of Military Justice; or in the case of the Church, a lawful order is any order that does not contradict the Word of God. This is one reason why it is so important that we spend time in the Word of God. Ignorance of the law is not a valid defense in any courtroom in the world, and neither will it be one when we stand before the Lord on Judgment Day. We are not going to be able to stand before the Lord and tell Him we did not know we were sinning when we had ample opportunity to read His Word whenever we liked.

So what are some examples of a lawful order that we might hear from a leader in our church? Being told to show up for a work day at the church would be a lawful order. Being told to arrive at church on time would also constitute a lawful order. Like the military, a disciple of Christ is held to a higher standard than those within the world. They must obey the laws of their government as well as the laws of the Kingdom of God. If we can not obey our nation's leaders then how are we to believe we can obey the Lord? It is a hard pill to swallow, but this is only because disobedience has become such a common occurrence in our society.

The dangers of disobedience within the Church are even more dangerous than those faced in the SEAL Teams. First, we are talking about sin, plain and simple. Many people in the Church, myself included, have judged sin in the past much like the secular community. They might say, "Well, that small sin is not so bad. After all, I am not killing anyone." But is this true? Every time we sin, we are killing our spirit and separating ourselves from God, not to speak of what it does to the Body of Christ.

I have heard people in the Church say that the God of the New Testament is merciful and not a harsh judge. I agree wholeheartedly that He is a God of infinite mercy, but He also is a righteous judge. Hebrews 10:26–31 describes our situation should we continue in our disobedience to the Father after having received the knowledge of truth. It describes it as "*insulting the Spirit of grace.*" It also says there

> "no longer remains a sacrifice for sins, but a certain terrifying expectation of judgment, and the fury of a fire which will consume the adversaries."

Remember Ananias and Sapphira in the book of Acts? They lied to the Holy Spirit, and it cost them their lives. Peter asked them, "*Why is it that you have agreed together to put the Spirit of the Lord to the test?*" I ask today, "Why is it we feel we can put the Spirit of the Lord to the test in our own lives?" I am not saying we should spend our days only looking for sin in the Body of Christ, so that we can sit in judgment of each other. But if sin exists, we must recognize the opportunity to help our brothers and sisters to identify the disobedience in their lives before their disobedience is handled by the Righteous Judge. God is a merciful Judge, and He has set up the Body of Christ in a way that allows us to show His mercy by helping our brothers and sisters to confess their sin and repent before they reach a point that demands accountability for their actions. I would much rather have any sin in my life pointed out to me by a member of my congregation, so that I might repent of it, rather than arrive at church some Sunday and drop dead as soon as I enter the building.

Peter gave Ananias and Sapphira a chance to repent, so they would not have to face the Holy Spirit's judgment. If we do not show love to the members of the Body of Christ by judging the sin in their lives, God will take care of His Body by removing the sin from it Himself. The Holy Spirit passed judgment on Ananias. After Peter told Sapphira she would be carried out as her husband, she also died. She did not die though until she was given a chance to repent. I do not believe Peter wanted her to die, but she did die because of her unwillingness to repent. I am just giving fair warning that His hand of mercy will not be on the Church forever. He will not allow us to live in disobedience forever. The Bible describes this individual as, "*The one who says, 'I have come to know Him,' and does not keep His commandments, is a liar, and the truth is not in him*" (1 John 2:4). He will have a white bride for His Son to come back to, and it can become white the easy way or the hard way. We are still under His hand of mercy, so I urge the Church to act now while we are still in boot camp; because once the Bride of Christ is purified, He will not allow it to be tainted again.

God's S.O.T. Teams will be working under a greater anointing of the Holy Spirit than ever witnessed in the world before. So great, I believe, they will not be able to walk with the blemish of sin in their lives. Paul challenged us to, *"Be imitators of me, just as I also am of Christ" (1 Corinthians 11:1).* To imitate means to follow as a model or to mimic. Another translation says we should follow him as he follows Christ. To follow means to pursue, obey, or keep one's attention fixed on.

The only two men in the Bible that I am aware of having ever given this command were Jesus and Paul. Jesus was able to give us this command because He was the Son of God and blameless before God. He is the perfect example. What gave Paul the right to give this command? At one point during his ministry, Paul proclaimed,

> "Not that I have already obtained it or have already become perfect, but I press on so that I may lay hold of that for which also I was laid hold of by Christ Jesus" (Philippians 3:12).

He admitted that he was not yet perfect, but that he was pressing on towards it. Had he finally been able to achieve living a life in perfect obedience to the Father just as Christ had? I believe so. If he had disobeyed the Lord even once after making this statement, he would be condoning his disobedience. How could he say we should follow him as he followed Christ? Christ never disobeyed the Father. If Paul was still living in disobedience, he should have said, "Follow Christ as I do." I have heard many people say, "I know the Bible says to live in perfect obedience, but I am not Christ. He was, after all, the Son of God and was conceived by the Holy Spirit." If what

I am saying about Paul is true, this argument holds no water. By his own account, Paul says,

> "For I am the least of the apostles, and not fit to be called an apostle, because I persecuted the church of God" (1 Corinthians 15:9).

He was a murderer and persecuted the Church before he was converted. He was not conceived by the Holy Spirit, and he was not the son of God. He was like the rest of us, or as he said, "*the least of the apostles.*" I am not aware of any other person, other than Christ or Paul, who has told us to pursue them or keep our eyes fixed on them and to live our lives exactly as they did. If Paul could live in perfect obedience then what excuse do we have? Paul is no longer with us, so all we have are his teachings, but Christ is still with us, at least in Spirit. We have the same example to follow in Christ as Paul did. We should be the ones now who say, "Be imitators of me, as I am of Christ."

Disobedience is rooted in selfishness and pride. We want to do something other than what is being asked of us to do. Why would someone choose to obey rather than disobey? It might be to avoid the consequence of disobedience. They do not want to get fired or thrown in jail. Why did Jesus obey the Father? It was because of His love for the Father that he obeyed even to the point of death, even death on a cross. Love is a much stronger motive for obedience than fear, but do not be deceived. The love of the Father will not keep His judgment from us forever if we continue to live in disobedience. We need to look at our lives and see if our love for Him motivates us to obey Him or not. In the past, I wanted to believe I loved the Father with my whole heart. I have had to rethink this belief though as I see the imperfection of disobedience in my life. It is not just obedience to the laws laid down for us by the Father, but it is a perfect obedience to His every word. God did not tell Moses he could not strike the rock in Kadesh. He simply told Moses to speak to the rock, and that was all. Moses spoke to the people, but he also struck the rock. Maybe, he became confused. After all, he struck the rock before in Rephidim. Maybe, because he was distracted by all the complaining people, he was just not paying close enough attention to God when he was told to just speak to the rock. No matter what the reason, he did not obey God perfectly because he acted in a way that God did not instruct him to act at that specific time and place.

I am not yet perfect either, but as Paul said,

> "I press on so that I may lay hold of that for which also I was laid hold of by Christ Jesus."

Why is disobedience not an issue in the SEAL Teams? We love our job and the SEAL community. We would not do anything that would bring shame to our unit or command. If need be, I would have died for anyone I have served with in the SEALs. How much more should we love the Father, Son, and Holy Spirit? How much more should we lay down our lives for our brothers and sisters in the Lord?

God's S.O.T. Teams will operate in this kind of love. They will live in absolute obedience to the Father because of their love for Him. They will only do what the Spirit tells them to do and speak only what the Spirit tells them to speak. They will live their lives as it is described in 1 Peter 4:11. It says:

> Whoever speaks, is to do so as one who is speaking the utterances of God; whoever serves is to do so as one who is serving by the strength which God supplies; so that in all things God may be glorified through Jesus Christ, to whom belongs the glory and dominion forever and ever. Amen.

For this reason, they will obey the authorities put over them in the Church because of their love for the Father and for each other. They will obey the authorities they live under in this world as long as they are not given unlawful orders.

Imagine what it will look like when the entire Body of Christ is acting in perfect obedience to the Father. When the enemies of God see this kind of obedience, they will flee before us. Why? I remember a true story I was once told that clearly makes this point. Even though some of the facts might be obscured slightly, the point is still well made.

Many years ago, there were two generals who were getting ready to face each other in battle. The invading general's army heavily outnumbered the defending general's forces by about 50 to 1. The outnumbered general realized he was facing extremely stiff odds. He petitioned for a meeting with the invading general. The invading general agreed to the meeting, and both generals brought along a contingent of soldiers. The meeting was held at the edge of an extremely high cliff overlooking the battle field. The two generals stood looking over the two armies below. The outnumbered general glanced over to the invading general and calmly asked him for his surrender. The invading general looked back towards the two armies and then with a slight grin replied that he had everything he needed to insure a sound victory. He would not be surrendering any time soon. The defending general turned and motioned to two of his lowest ranking soldiers standing near by. He ordered them to throw themselves off the cliff, smashing themselves into the gagged rocks below. Without a moments hesitation, the two soldiers ran towards the cliff and leaped over. The invading general peered over the side of the cliff in horror to see their lifeless bodies lying mangled at the bottom of the cliff. The defending general looked solemnly at the invading general and said, "Every soldier I have follows me in the same manner as what you have just witnessed." With a ghastly look upon his face the invading general turned to his soldiers and ordered their return home. He surrendered without a fight. Why? He knew the power that came with being able to command an army acting as one body; an army with one mind, one heart, and one purpose. He knew if the body followed the head in perfect obedience there was no army capable of standing in its way. There are more lessons that can be derived from this true story, but I only want to highlight the lesson of obedience. We will see amazing things begin to happen in the world when the Body of Christ obeys her King in all things just as the two soldiers obeyed their general even to a sacrificial death.

We have a big advantage over the New Testament believers like Paul. We have the Word of God to guide us. Many of the things Paul wrote about in the New Testament were taught to him directly by the Holy Spirit. That which took him many years to learn can now be read by us in just a few days. Of course, reading it and learning the lessons are two different things. But what would be easier to do? Would it be easier to rebuild a car's engine using a manual with pictures and specific instructions or having someone try to walk us through it over the phone when we do not even know what the parts are called or what they look like?

As these S.O.T. Teams begin living in perfect obedience to God, He will entrust them with visions of heaven and prophetic insight into things to come. The Light that is shining from their lives will guide the Body of Christ during the darkest times and usher in the end time Church. It has been said that if the military was a sword, the Special Operation Teams in the military are the tip of the sword. The same can be said about the Church. If the Church is a sword, these S.O.T. Teams in the Church are the also at the tip of that sword. The tip is the sharpest point on the blade, but it is also the weakest. SEAL Team operators are very sharp, and they can cause a lot of damage to an enemy, but if they make a mistake and are compromised on a mission, their lives could be at risk. If these men and women of God make the mistake of allowing disobedience into their lives, they will become compromised, and they will suffer the consequences of their actions. Obedience will be the key, and that obedience must be motivated by love. The dangers and consequences are real, but so is the glory that will be given to our King when we live perfectly obedient lives.

Chapter VIII

There is no "I" in Team

I would say, without a doubt, one of the most important concepts a young SEAL will learn is the value of teamwork. This is the very reason they are called the SEAL Teams. John Donne, a colonial preacher, once suggested, "No man is an island unto himself." The same thing can be said about the SEAL Teams. From the very first day of BUD/S training, a candidate learns that if he is going to make it through the training, he must rely not only on his own abilities but also on that of his teammates.

Military boot camp teaches this concept too, but BUD/S takes it one step further by fabricating it into the lifestyle of the student. After a student graduates BUD/S training, they will never again look at any task in life as an individual challenge. If there are other people with them, they will try to pull everyone together and use the team's strengths to accomplish the task. The idea is that four eyes are better than two. Of course, it helps when everyone is on the same page. The larger the team, the harder it is for everyone to have the same vision.

One way BUD/S training bonds the students together is through suffering, and I can personally testify there is no shortage of suffering. For this reason, the SEAL Teams are more like a brotherhood than a work place. I can run across a SEAL anywhere in the world, and immediately, we become best friends. We share a common bond in the suffering we both experienced while going through BUD/S. It is a bond only another SEAL could ever understand. It is like the bond between a mother and child. Only a mother could truly ever understand the strength of that bond.

There is a motto we use at BUD/S to drill the concept of teamwork into the mind of the candidate. "There is no 'I' in Team." Obviously, it means more than just the grammatical fact that the letter "I" is not in the word "Team." The idea is that within a team environment we can not exist as individuals. Instead, we must behave as one body with one vision. We must act in the best interest of each other rather than the best interest of ourselves.

I remember an event which happened to me in BUD/S, capable of shining some light on this subject. It was during a part of the training known as "Hell Week." Training events in BUD/S are called evolutions. This evolution takes place during the fifth week of training. It begins on Sunday night, and it lasts until Friday evening. During this period of training, a candidate might receive a total of four hour of sleep if they are lucky. Usually, the sleep comes in fitful naps taken whenever and wherever you can. That is a total of five days with only about four hours of sleep. During "Hell Week," the candidates are continually harassed and put through mind numbing and physically depleting evolutions one right after another.

The plan is to simulate the stress of combat without putting the candidate's life at too much of a risk. Candidates drop out like flies during this phase of training. A class of ninety students will lose, on average, around sixty students during this week.

The particular event I am referring to was sometime during Wednesday night of "Hell Week." We had already been going nonstop for over eighty hours, and we were all extremely tired and extremely cold. It was winter and the water in the San Diego Bay was "bone cold." It is called "bone cold" because the temperature of your body drops so low that it feels like your bones get cold. When someone is awake for that long their body becomes more susceptible to hypothermia than when they are well rested. We had been placed into the bay, and we were told to sit down until the water came up to our necks. During "Hell Week," we have to wear large lifejackets, so we will not drown if we fall asleep while we are in the water. They also serve the purpose of bringing misery into the candidate's life by rubbing against the body, causing open wounds to form that burn and irritate us the entire week. After we sat down in the water, they told us to lock our arms together so that no one would drift off into the bay by themselves.

We were then told we were going to play a game. Oh boy, a game! Trust me, the games we played were not meant to be enjoyable. An instructor would whisper something into the candidate's ear on the end of the line, and they would have to pass it on down to the next candidate until it had made it all the way down to the last man. When the information had been passed to the last man he would shout out loud what had been passed to him. If the information was exactly the same as that of the instructor's, we would be allowed to exit the frigid water.

If it was slightly different, even by one syllable, we would play the game again. Usually, the information would come down the line as a combination of different numbers or some other abstract comment that would be meant to throw us off.

We played this game for almost an hour when I realized I could not remember why I was there. One of the signs of hyperthermia is that the victim will lose their ability to think rationally. I knew I was cold, but I could not understand what was happening to me. Somehow I knew I should not get out of the water, so I just sat there and waited. I do not remember anything else after that moment. My next recollection of the events of that night was that I was being drug down the road between two of my fellow classmates. They were trying to get me to walk on my own. Everything I know about that night was told to me by my teammates. They said I just kept mumbling over and over, "I'm so cold, I can't think!" I was still awake, and my eyes were still open. The students next to me in the water had been keeping an eye on me, and they were helping me during the game by passing the information around me. They were about to tell the instructor staff that I had hyperthermia, but right at that moment we were allowed to exit the water.

In BUD/S, one of the greatest fears is that we will be rolled back to a different class and have to go through the training again. Rollbacks usually occur when someone becomes injured, or they become so badly sick that they can not continue the training. My teammates did not want this to happen to me, so they helped me through the evolution until I could continue on my own. This might seem kind of extreme, but it is necessary that we learn that in a real world combat environment our teammates are sometimes the only ones we can count on.

I found out later on that hypothermia would not have gotten me rolled back. I would have just been warmed back up and put back with my class. Of course, I did not know this at the time, so I was very grateful for what they had done for me. They could have easily just handed me over to the instructors, but they did not. They chose to carry my weight because of the bond we had established between our team. We had become one body, and every time we lost someone the entire class felt it.

The SEAL Teams exist within the U.S. military. They fall under all the laws and rules applying to that institution, but they are much more than that. It is the personal bonds that are established allowing a unity and cohesiveness to form that I have never experienced anywhere else in this world. A SEAL would do anything for his brother-in-arms. They are closer than family, and even though I have not met every one of them, I still feel a connection with them. When I hear that a SEAL has been killed or is missing in action, it does something to me. Our relationships are almost like that of a twin. I have worked so closely with my fellow SEALs that a simple glance can tell me what they are thinking. We get to know each other well enough, so that we can almost predetermine each others actions. This unity is one of the main reasons we have always been so successful.

I do not feel this kind of unity within the Church today. I believe it should not only be felt among members in the Church, but it should also be outwardly evident to those in the world. Remember the SEAL Team's motto for teamwork? "There is no 'I' in Team?" Well, the Father has also given us a motto in the Church dating all the way back to the book of Leviticus. Jesus repeated it again in the New Testament, *"You shall love your neighbor as yourself" (Matthew 22:39).* We should spend as much time looking out for the interests of others as we do ourselves. I believe Jesus took this even further when He told us to deny ourselves, take up our cross, and follow Him. He taught us to be servants of all, and so we must be.

The Church has access to a bonding power the world can not experience. This bonding power is the Holy Spirit. Through the Holy Spirit, we can be unified in the suffering of Christ. The Scripture says in Romans:

> The Spirit Himself testifies with our spirit that we are children of God, and if children, heirs also, heirs of God and fellow heirs with Christ, if indeed we suffer with Him so that we may also be glorified with Him. For I consider that the sufferings of this present time are not worthy to be compared with the glory that is to be revealed to us. (Romans 8:16–18)

Jesus' heart is for the unification of His body. He prayed and asked the Father to let us be one as He and the Father were one. He told the Father,

> "The glory which You have given Me I have given to them, that they may be one, just as We are one" (John 17:22).

This issue is so important to the Lord it is mentioned in the Scriptures over and over again. It is one of the last prayers Jesus prayed before His death. This principle of unity applies to the entire Church, and if God has to allow suffering in order to bind our hearts together within the Church, we can be sure that He will.

This kind of unity will be an absolute necessity for God's S.O.T. Teams. It may be necessary for one member to know what the other member is thinking and for both members to know what the Spirit is saying. I believe, if they both have the mind of Christ and they all are in the Spirit, this will be possible.

The Bible says our thoughts are only known to ourselves. Another man can not read our thoughts. It says,

> "For who among men knows the thoughts of a man except the spirit of the man which is in him? Even so the thoughts of God no one knows except the Spirit of God" (1 Corinthians 2:11).

Other than our own spirit, God alone knows the thoughts of man. The scripture says,

> "For the word of God is living and active and sharper than any two-edged sword, and piercing as far as the division of soul and spirit, of both joints and marrow, and able to judge the thoughts and intentions of the heart" (Hebrews 4:12).

We know that the Word of God is God because in John it says, "*In the beginning was the Word, and the Word was with God, and the Word was God" (John 1:1)*

Our spiritual enemies can not know what we are thinking, unless of course, they put the thoughts there themselves, or we verbalize them with our mouths. It is a way to communicate with the Lord without having anyone tap into your communication lines. When we are on a mission in the SEALs, we use hand signals a lot. This allows us to communicate without being heard by the enemy. Our ability to communicate with the Lord through the Spirit is similar to hand signals. It is a silent means of communication.

Another benefit of praying in the Spirit is that the Spirit knows exactly what to say on our behalf. We are told:

> In the same way the Spirit also helps our weakness; for we do not know how to pray as we should, but the Spirit Himself intercedes for us with groanings too deep for words; and He who searches the hearts knows what the mind of the Spirit is, because He intercedes for the saints according to the will of God. (Romans 8:26–27)

Speaking in tongues is another way that we can communicate with the Lord and still remain clandestine. I believe there is a language spoken in heaven that we on earth can not understand. In Revelations, it says,

> "And I heard a voice from heaven, as the voice of many waters, and as the voice of a great thunder: and the voice which I heard was as the voice of harpers harping with their harps" (Revelations 14:2.)

The Lord can give us the ability to speak an unknown language, but it is entirely up to Him.

He can also choose to allow someone here on earth to be able to interpret that spoken word. The ability to interpret unknown tongues is mentioned in 1 Corinthians when it says,

> "and to another the effecting of miracles, and to another prophecy, and to another the distinguishing of spirits, to another various kinds of tongues, and to another the interpretation of tongues" (1 Corinthians 12:10).

In the military, we use encrypted communication devices. These send information over an open channel, but it is garbled. If we do not have the codes on the receiving end, we will not be able to understand what information is being sent. Tongues are an encryption device used by the Father. It is another way that we can communicate with each other without the enemy knowing what is going on. If the Lord gives us the ability to understand the tongues then He has given us the codes needed to decipher the message. In our military units, encryption codes are only used for a short while, maybe for only one mission, and then they must be changed. This keeps the enemy from being able to figure out the codes and using them against us. God can give the ability to translate a spoken tongue, and when we no longer need the ability, remove it from us. Since the Holy Spirit gives us the ability to speak in tongues, and He knows best how to petition the Father, we can use tongues to pray out loud the exact words the Holy Spirit wants us to speak. This has to be one of the most efficient ways to pray. I reiterate the words Paul spoke, *"Now I wish that you all spoke in tongues" (1 Corinthians 14:5).*

In order to communicate in this way, the communicators are going to have to be one with the power source. If we are on different types of radios it will not work. God's S.O.T. Teams are going to be working behind enemy lines, and they are going to have to have a way to call in support should it be needed. Fortunately, they will have the Holy Spirit with them at all times, so there should not be any concern. As humans though, we sometimes need others to build us up or support us. This bonding is described in Ecclesiastes when it states,

> "And if one can overpower him who is alone, two can resist him. A cord of three strands is not quickly torn apart" (Ecclesiastes 4:12).

Paul may have asked for Timothy and Silas to join him for this very reason. Imagine if Paul could have just prayed silently in his heart asking the Lord to send Timothy and Silas with the reason for his request. The Spirit could have let Timothy and Silas know what was being requested, have Timothy and Silas go to Paul, and the enemy would have been none the wiser. The Lord gives us instructions, and the enemy would love to intercept those messages. Do not be deceived, there is a war raging all around us. Just because you can not see it does not mean it does not exist.

Secrecy is a tool used by SEALs in order to surprise the enemy. God's S.O.T. Teams will use this method as well. Let me give an example. If the Lord wanted me to go to a hospital and heal everyone in it, would the enemy have the ability to stop me? Sure they would. They could send the spirit of doubt and fear to the hospital ahead of me, so even if I believed, my faith alone would not be enough. Jesus ran into this problem when the people in his home town did not believe. It says in Matthew 13:58 that Jesus did not perform many miracles in His home town because of their unbelief. This is one reason that leads me to believe God will implement this spiritual type of communication between these team members.

There is a saying in the military when it comes to security issues. It is the "need to know" concept. If we do not need to know something, chances are we will not know. God works in the Church in the same way. He does not let everyone know what is going on because we do not all need to know. God has established His own checks and balances in the Church, like His apostles and prophets, to keep everything in line with His will. This goes back to the chapter on obedience. We do not need to be second guessing everything our leaders tell us. As long as they coincide with the scriptures then we need to obey and let God handle the rest. I am sure He is capable of taking care of His own body.

I hope this point is made clear because when people work under a great anointing of the Holy Spirit, they tend to be privy to information the rest of us do not receive. If we are going to be a part of this team, we are going to have to realize that we will not be able to share everything, with everyone, no matter how exciting it might be. We can only pass on the information the Lord tells us too. If the Lord shows us something, so exciting we can hardly stand it, we must be very careful in how we use that knowledge. This is where having a team member with us comes in handy. In the SEAL Teams, we are all given the same security clearances. Many of the missions we are involved in, we can share with other SEALs. It gives us an outlet to share our feelings. We can not share those feelings and thoughts with our families and friends who are outside our community because of security issues. Sometimes, we are given a mission with an elevated security clearance, and the only ones we can talk to about it are those which are directly involved with. In reference to our spiritual lives, Jesus says:

> So when you give to the poor, do not sound a trumpet before you, as the hypocrites do in the synagogues and in the streets, so that they may be honored by men. Truly I say to you, they have their reward in full. But when you give to the poor, do not let your left hand know what your right hand is doing, so that your giving will be in secret; and your Father who sees what is done in secret will reward you. (Matthew 6:2–4)

Not everything God has us do needs to be public information. There are times for secrecy, and there are times for things to be manifested. Either way, great knowledge brings great responsibility. Being part of a cohesive team helps with this responsibility.

The unity that will be established in God's S.O.T. Teams will enable the team members to work efficiently and with great effectiveness. It will come at a price though. A complete and utter sacrifice of our selfish ambitions will have to be placed upon the altar before we will be admitted entrance into this community. God's desires can be the only plan of action. This will allow us to be of one mind and one spirit. There can not be any lone warriors in this fight. All for One, and One for All!

Chapter IX

The Perfect Soldier

One thing I have learned by going through BUD/S is that I am capable of much more than I think I am. In the SEAL Teams, we are taught to pay attention to the details. Another word that describes this attention is perfection. A determined extremist who does not strive for perfection is heading for disaster. We must be highly skilled in our craft to be excellent at it. The desire to be excellent alone is not enough.

Navy SEALs are definitely perfectionists. Living a lifestyle pursuing perfection is different than being considered a master craftsman. We are, after all, "Jacks of all trades and masters of none." A master craftsman knows everything about a specific craft or skill. A perfectionist might not know everything about a specific craft, but what they do know they do to perfection. For example, a master weapons handler in small arms would know everything about every small arms weapon ever made. I am not a master weapons handler in small arms, but as a perfectionist, I can take apart and put back together an M-16 rifle blindfolded and in record time.

We are taught from the very beginning there is no such thing as a perfect plan, but we always strive to plan the perfect mission. If we set our goals high enough we might become disappointed, but it is better to be disappointed for missing a lofty goal than to settle with mediocrity. Great accomplishments are achieved by those who aspire towards excellence.

SEALs have the honor of being called the "best" at what we do because we do not settle for second place. One well known creed in BUD/S is "second place is the first loser." I know this probably sounds harsh, but in combat, second place is the guy who does not get to go home to see his family. This is a way of life for us. SEALs are extremely competitive by nature. Being the best is one of the reasons we can be called upon for any type of mission. A football coach would not want to put their second string quarterback into an important game would they? The same can be said for the military. Competition is rooted into the BUD/S program, but its candidates are usually extremely competitive individuals long before arriving on our quarterdeck.

In today's society, competition has been frowned upon when it involves youth sports or other activities. Our youth are taught it is better to have fun than to win. I agree that when competition is based upon pride and selfish ambitions it can cause harm. On the other hand, when we engage in competition out of obedience to the Father, we bring Him glory. The world has no concept of living for the glory of God, and I do not expect them to understand this concept, but I do believe the Church should understand it. When we only teach our children about competition from a secular understanding, we do them a great disservice by allowing them to be lulled into a life of mediocrity.

I remember a movie called "Chariots of Fire" that came out when I was younger. It was based upon a true story, and I encourage anyone who has not seen it to make the effort to do so. It was about a Scottish rugby player named Eric Liddell, who lived during the early 1900's. He grew up in a missionary family. He had plans to follow his father onto the mission field, but he was also a very gifted runner. Because he was so gifted, he had an opportunity to participate in the Olympic Games in Athens. His sister Jenny wanted him to give up the silly notion of competing in athletics and quickly get onto the mission field because she thought the competition was ruining his walk with the Lord. I will never forget what he said to her. He looked at her in all gentleness and said, "Jenny, God made me fast for a reason, and when I run I can feel His pleasure." He went on to the Olympics where He did indeed bring glory to the Lord. I do not want to ruin the end of the story, but the glory he brought the Lord was not only because of his running. I read his biography after I watched the movie, and one thing the movie does not tell us is that immediately after finishing his race, he left for China to meet his family on the mission field. He was killed on the mission field as a martyr during the Boxer Rebellions. Every time this story is told, the Lord receives glory. Just think about it. If he would not have trained to be the best, he would have not made the Olympic team. If he had not competed in the Olympics, the movie would not have been filmed. If I would have not seen the movie, I would not have read his biography. If I would not have read his biography, I would not have been able to write about his death as a martyr. Think of all the glory that would not have gone to the Father if this chain of events had not occurred.

At high levels of competition the small details are the difference between first and second place. Those who do not want to settle for second place seek out those small differences in order to perform better the next time. If someone is satisfied in just having fun, why would they try to better themselves? We tell our children to do their best, but how are they to judge what that is? How does a child or even an adult for that matter, know what their limitations are? Competition gives us a playing field in which to judge our performance and measure our improvements and growth.

When I went to BUD/S, I thought I knew my limitations. I quickly learned that I was wrong. I was shown that my mind and body could take more punishment than humanly thought possible. I also learned by raising the bar I could push myself harder because my mind was not telling me to stop. I had competed in athletics for most of my life, and I had tested myself in many different physical challenges prior to attending BUD/S. I thought I would be able to tell when I was giving it my all. Fortunately, the BUD/S instructors would not let me stop at my predetermined limits. When I thought I had nothing left, they asked me for more. My determination helped me to keep going when I thought I was on empty, but by striving for excellence, I was able to set higher standards and push my limitations much higher than I had imagined possible.

How do we judge excellence? The word excellence comes from the root word excel. Webster's New Thesaurus says the word excel "implies preeminence in achievement or quality and may suggest superiority to all other." If someone is the best in the world at something, would we say they excel or are excellent at it? If they are excellent then what is just below them? Can it also be called excellent? I think not. During competition, we are placing ourselves in an environment where we can be pushed towards excellence. If we can see that we are not the best then we are given a goal to shoot for. If we are told we do not need to be the best then we are being taught to settle for less than excellence. In other words, we are settling for mediocrity.

I remember a time during my SEAL training when this push for excellence reaped my platoon many rewards. It was during winter (funny how it always seems to be winter) and my platoon was being sent to South Korea to partake in some training exercises with the South Korean Army. I was the point man in my platoon, and it regularly fell upon me to plan our insertions and extractions for missions that we might be tasked with. The mission we were given on this particular evening was a training mission to test the South Korean Army's ability to defend their coastal waterways. In many ways, these events were our place of competition. The best man won, and someone always lost.

We inserted into the operational area using our Special Boat Units, high speed vessels used to transport SEAL platoons long distances. This method required me and one other teammate from my platoon to swim into the beach to find out if it was safe for the rest of my platoon to come ashore. It was extremely dark outside because a heavy cloud cover was blocking the moon and starlight from above. When I reached the beach, I noticed a group of South Korean Army personnel patrolling the coastline. Because of the emanate threat from North Korea, the South Korean Army is always on alert, and they will usually shoot first and ask questions later. I was not worried though because they would have been notified that we were coming. They would be looking for us, but they would not be using live ammunition.

I did not care if it was a real mission or a training mission. Either way, I was going to treat it as though it were for real. I was going to get us into the target and out of the target without being detected. I wanted to win! I moved in close enough to see that they were eating oysters around a fire, and I could hear their conversation. I could not understand what they were saying though because I did not speak the Korean language well enough.

I held my platoon at bay while we waited for the South Korean Army personnel to leave the beach. They were not our target, and there was no reason to become involved with them unless it became absolutely necessary. Finally, after what seemed like forever, they left, and we were able to continue on towards the target. A few hours into the mission we noticed a vehicle moving rapidly towards out position with its headlights flashing and blasting its horn every few seconds. I thought we were compromised, and we dove behind cover to avoid being spotted. As the vehicle made it closer, we could hear someone yelling in English for a "training time out," a break from a training evolution because of safety concerns.

We walked out to meet the vehicle and quickly learned the grim news that sparked the urgent request for a "training time out." Somehow, the South Korean forces in the area had not been notified that we were coming, and they were carrying live rounds in their weapons, not a good combination. We were then asked if we had seen any South Koreans, and when we told the training personnel just how close we had been, they were very relieved to find out nothing had happened but not nearly as much as I was. If I had approached the mission as just another training mission and had not tried to "win," there is a good chance they could have spotted us. If this would have occurred, the outcome would not have been very pleasant. By striving for excellence, my platoon was successful and stayed safe in an environment that was very unsafe.

Our journey through this world is a competition. Paul agrees with this statement when he says,

> "Do you not know that those who run in a race all run, but only one receives the prize? Run in such a way that you may win" (1 Corinthians 9:24).

Believe it or not, we are competing as we race through this life in the pursuit of Christ and His kingdom. What is the prize? Paul says,

> "I press on toward the goal for the prize of the upward call of God in Christ Jesus" (Philippians 3:14).

We are not necessarily competing against each other, as much as we are competing against Christ Himself. How can this be? Have you ever seen how a younger sibling will compete with an older sibling in an attempt to try and measure up to the older sibling's accomplishments? Christ is our elder brother, and Paul says we are to be conformed into His image. He describes this conformation by saying,

> "For those whom He foreknew, He also predestined to become conformed to the image of His Son, so that He would be the firstborn among many brethren" (Romans 8:29).

There is only One who is truly excellent; He is our King and older brother Jesus. We are to be like Him. We are to try to figure out how He lived His life and live ours the same way. Jesus is running in first place, and we are trying to fine tune our race so that we can finish along side Him. Is this possible? With the grace of God in our lives it is. Like I said before, I believe Paul made it. He said in 2 Timothy, "*I have fought the good fight, I have finished the course, I have kept the faith.*" Obviously, he was not speaking about his death because he was not being put to death right at that moment. I believe he had reached the point where he was like Christ, living in perfect obedience to the Father.

Being a perfectionist in the Kingdom of God does not mean we are master craftsman either. There is only one Master in the Kingdom of God, and He can not be surpassed by those who serve Him. We can be perfectionist though when it comes to loving, obeying, and being unified with the Body of Christ. The Master is perfect in all things. He is omnipotent and omnipresent. He is not only our Master but our Creator. He wants us to be like Him, just as a son who wants to be like his father. We must try to be perfect in love because He is perfect in love. We must try to be perfect in obedience because Jesus is perfect in obedience to the Father. We must try to be perfect in unity because the Father and Son are perfectly unified.

Our perfect obedience must be lived out all the way until the end. Moses lost his chance to enter the Promised Land towards the end of his life. We must stay steadfast until the end and not allow the enemy to rob us of our reward that is waiting for us in heaven. Jesus was obedient to the Father unto death, even death on a cross. The enemy attacked Jesus until the very moment He gave up His life. He was ridiculed by the enemy around Him as they yelled out for Him to deliver Himself.

I remember a time in high school when I had an opportunity to learn this lesson the hard way. I participated in track and field, but unlike Eric Liddell, I competed for myself and for my own ambitions. I had been preparing for an important invitational meet being held at the end of our season. I trained hard for this meet, and when the time came, I felt that I was ready.

Throughout the meet our team stayed close to the lead, and when it came time for the last race of the meet, we were in second place by only a few points. If we could win the last race we would capture the first place trophy overall. It was a relay, and I had the honor of running the last leg.

The race was tight with the lead changing hands a few times. Finally, it came down to my leg. I was running the 800 meter leg in the medley race, and my archrival was running against me. He had beaten me all season, and even though the races had been close, I had never been able to get the better of him. Going into the last leg he had a ten meter lead on me. I took the baton from my teammate and began the chase. I quickly closed the gap because I did not want him to get too far ahead of me, and then I just sat off his shoulder and waited for my chance to make my move. Going down the backstretch of the final lap, I decided it was now or never. I knew that if I did not blow by him, he would manage to stick with me and out kick me in the end. Because he had a really good finish, I made sure that when I passed him, I did it with authority. I was not sure if I could keep it up for the rest of the race at the pace that I was running, but I had to try. I put my head down and just ran. I did not hear the roar of the crowd, and I did not see anything except the finish line.

As a runner, I was taught to never look back for

the runner behind you. It shows weakness, and it gives the runner behind you an opportunity to pass you on the opposite side of where you are looking. I could not help myself. Going down the final stretch I just had to look. I looked over my right shoulder, but I did not see him. Fearing that he was passing me on the opposite side, I quickly looked over my left shoulder. Amazingly, he was nowhere to be found.

I crossed the tape in first place with about a fifteen meters lead over my archrival. We had won, and I was ecstatic! I threw the baton into the air in jubilation, and ran off the track to begin the celebration. I could not believe it. We had pulled the upset of the season, and I had smashed my archrival all in one blow.

My coach made his way over to our team, which by now had piled on top of me. His facial expression was not one that I was expecting to see because it was a dismal look that was staring down on me as I laid half buried by my teammates. I had no idea why he was not celebrating with us in our moment of glory, or at least offering his congratulations to his star athlete—namely me. After all, I had just won the first place trophy for us, right? Wrong! "There seems to have been a ruling on the track that is not going to go in our favor," my coach grimly announced. He informed me that our team had been disqualified because I had thrown the baton before I stepped off the track. The real slap in the face came when I found out we had dropped below third place overall as well. We finished out of the trophies all together because we had not received any points for the race due to the disqualification. Not only had I lost the race for the team, but I had lost them any chance of receiving a team trophy whatsoever! Needless to say, the trip home was pretty quiet. The lesson I learned that day is that a race is not over until I am holding the prize in my hands.

While we will never surpass Christ in this race we call life, we should try to be just as He is. Christ is perfection. Jesus taught us how to live, and at the end of one of His sermons, He made a statement that I believe was prophetic. If we lived our lives the way He taught us to be, we would be perfect. He simply said, *"Therefore you are to be perfect, as your heavenly Father is perfect" (Matthew 5:48).* He requires, no, demands perfection in us just as He and the Father are perfect. He is speaking of a perfect love, perfect obedience, and perfect unity. These three things can be summed up in the two greatest commandments Jesus identified in the gospels. In order to live them, we must be in perfect obedience and demonstrating a perfect love. If we do this, it will lead us into a perfect unity with all those who do the same.

We are to love the Father perfectly just as Jesus loves Him. What does that look like? Jesus said we should love the Father with our whole heart, soul, mind, and strength. We can not surpass perfect love. Therefore, we can not surpass Christ. What would be a perfect marathon? I would have to say that theoretically a time of zero would qualify. While a time of zero could be matched, theoretically, it would be impossible to better it. In the same way, we can not better the love of Christ, but we can and should try to emulate it. I believe we can finish our race hand in hand with Christ.

Perfection is a characteristic of God. I love the way He is described as in Deuteronomy when it says,

> "The Rock! His work is perfect, For all His ways are just; A God of faithfulness and without injustice, Righteous and upright is He" (Deuteronomy 32:4).

We can see His perfection in the Old Testament as He gave the requirements for the building of the temple. He gave exact measurements and told them exactly what kind of material to use. He gave them detailed instruction on how a high priest was to prepare himself for entry into the Holy of Holies. He told Noah exactly how to build the ark and what to take on the ark. Just look at nature. Our bodies have exactly what they need to live on this planet. The earth is exactly as far from the sun as it needs to be to keep us warm and sustain life. Everything around us is exact and screams of perfection! Perfection is what He wants to see in us, His creation, and His children.

I believe Satan knows it is possible, and this is why he tries so hard to get us to believe it is alright to be mediocre. He knows that if we can be trained to believe this then we will also believe it is alright to live a mediocre life for the Lord. He tells us part of the truth, so we will believe him. But he never tells us all of the truth, or we would see him for the liar that he is. He tells us it is alright to sin because God is a merciful God, and He will forgive us.

It is true that God is merciful and forgiving, but like Paul said in Romans,

> "Are we to continue in sin that grace might increase? May it never be! How shall we who died to sin still live in it?" (Romans 6:1).

What Satan does not tell us is that God has called us to live in righteousness, dedicating ourselves to a life of perfect obedience. It is clearly stated in the scriptures:

> The one who says, 'I have come to know Him,' and does not keep His commandments, is a liar, and the

> truth is not in him; but whoever keeps His word, in him the love of God has truly been perfected. By this we know that we are in Him: the one who says he abides in Him ought himself to walk in the same manner as He walked. (1 John 2:4–6)

As far as I can tell, the Church has overlooked this truth, and she has taken the enemy's bait, hook, line, and sinker. Our King will not allow this deception to continue for too much longer.

God is looking for those who will be willing to throw off this mediocrity which has become so evident in the Church and begin living lives of perfect love, perfect obedience, perfect unity, and excellence for the Kingdom of God. He wants us to live excellent lives so that the world might see the excellence, and our lives might bring glory to the Lord. We are further instructed in the New Testament:

> Beloved, I urge you as aliens and strangers to abstain from fleshly lusts which wage war against the soul. Keep your behavior excellent among the Gentiles, so that in the thing in which they slander you as evildoers, they may because of your good deeds, as they observe them, glorify God in the day of visitation. (1 Peter 2:11–13)

Many assume SEALs are arrogant and prideful people, and God's S.O.T. Teams will most likely have to deal with the same accusations. Those who choose to live their lives in this manner will have to walk continually in the love of God. Unfortunately, there will be those who will say these individuals are being nothing more than arrogant and self righteous. The enemy will try to use those who are closest to us to defeat us, and without the perfect love of God in our hearts, we might succumb to the slings and arrows that are flung at us.

Until the Church is cleansed from sin and the white Bride of Christ has risen up to stand in the earth, we will see what was spoken of in Jude. This was in reference to those individuals within the church who had *"crept in unnoticed."* We are reminded of the words spoken by the apostles of our Lord Jesus Christ when they said:

> In the last time there shall be mockers, following after their own ungodly lusts. These are the ones who cause divisions, worldly-minded, devoid of the Spirit. But you, beloved, building yourselves up on your most holy faith; praying in the Holy Spirit; keep yourselves in the love of God, waiting anxiously for the mercy of our Lord Jesus Christ to eternal life. And have mercy on some, who are doubting; save others, snatching them out of the fire; and on some have mercy with fear, hating even the garment polluted by the flesh. (Jude 1:17–24)

This will continue to happen until those individuals within the Church, who doubt in their own ability to live perfect lives, realize it is possible for them to live this way as well. God is looking for someone to live as an example on the earth the same way His Son did. The same way Paul did.

Conclusion

As a Navy SEAL recruiter, I spoke with many young men about becoming Navy SEALs. I would tell them the good, the bad, and the ugly. I would tell them the qualifications and what would be expected of them if they joined the program. I would dispel false rumors and give them enough truthful information about the program so that they could make an informed decision about joining. Usually, by the end of our discussion, they would respond in one of the following three ways: 1.) They would want the program more than life itself and stop at nothing to get it! 2.) They would think it was really interesting but they would have to think about it for awhile before making any decisions. 3.) They would say I was crazy and try to escape out of the back window.

Any of the three responses were fine by me. I only wanted those who fell under the first category anyways. It all boiled down to whether they had it in them or not. If I felt that they did not have a strong enough desire, I would tell them so. If I was wrong, they would let me know fairly quickly just as I did for my recruiter. I considered this my litmus test, and the results were usually pretty accurate. If they did not respond by saying, "Just try and stop me!" or something along those lines, I knew they would probably never pursue it again. No one who actually returned after thinking about it for more than twenty-four hours ever made it through the program either.

While these rules did apply to the applicants who I spoke with about the Navy SEALs, they do not necessarily apply in the exact same way to the applicants for God's S.O.T. Teams. Why not? Well, the applicants who I spoke with about the Navy SEALs were the way they were from birth. Some of them had it in them and some of them did not. If they had the character in them at birth but lost it along the way, it would be extremely difficult for them to get those gifts to resurface. While it would not be impossible, it would be very difficult. If they never had it, they were out of luck.

A born-again believer, on the other hand, has a special advantage. When we are born again, the Lord awakens gifts within us which were either laying dormant all our lives or might have been snuffed out by the enemy at a younger age. If He put those gifts inside us for this specific purpose, we can be sure He will get out of us what He has put into us. We might feel like we do not have these gifts simply because we have never acted this way during any of our natural life. For example, we might feel like we have never been a very determined individual, so we figure we must not be called to be one of these forerunners. This might be the very same lie the enemy has told us our whole life just to keep us from using the gifts the Lord has built into us before we were even born. If by reading this book, we have even a spark of desire to answer this call then we must pray to the Giver of the gifts and ask Him to manifest these gifts in our own life. Like I said before, if the Lord knows we truly want to obey His voice and fulfill His plans for our lives, He will be faithful to guide us.

The twenty-four hour period that I gave my SEAL candidates for making their enlistment decision does not necessarily apply to those who might be interested in a career as a S.O.T. Team member in God's Army. As born-again believers, we might not know what gifts have actually been given to us when we were created, so this might take a little more time and definitely a lot of prayer in order to allow the Lord to make His purpose for our lives clear to us. If we do not seek Him though, we will not find Him. The Bible says if we knock the door will be opened, and if we seek Him then we will find Him.

That is not to say we can not feel the passion for this calling right away either. Some of us might know the second we are shown this road that it is the road we were meant to travel down. To those who know right now or have already known for awhile, my advice is to act quickly. Time is a precious commodity, and we will need to have as many seasoned veterans as possible in the field to pave the way for the rest of the Church as they begin to follow.

There is a growing need in the world today for Special Operation Teams to take on a larger role in combating foreign enemy powers. The Body of Christ is also in need of having these forerunners who I have spoken about to take on a larger role in combating the spiritual enemies which threaten the Church. For those of us who know we are called to serve in this way, we need to act now if we want to be a part of this next and possibly last great move of the Spirit within the earth.

As the perfecting of the saints occurs, we will see a special grace from the Lord fall upon the Church which will allow the rest of the Body of Christ to follow. It has to start with those of us who are called to be a part of God's S.O.T. Teams. If the twelve spies had all come back with a good report, I believe the Children of Israel would have followed them through the Jordan River and into the Promised Land that very day! Because the twelve spies did not answer the call that God had ordained them for, the children of Israel missed out on the opportunity to see the promises of God answered during their life time. If we do not answer this call, then just like the children of Israel, we will have to wait for the next generation to enter the Promised Land. I, for one, will answer the call today just as Joshua and Caleb did thousands of years ago. My prayer is that all those who are called for this purpose will do the same.

As a disciple of Christ, we should all want to be just as He is. This desire is all we need to begin our journey down this high and narrow road because upon Christ's return all of those who have persevered until the end will be a part of the white and spotless Bride of Christ. The only question that remains is what role will we play within this end time Church? Will we be leading the way, or will we be following? The choice is up to us.

Scriptures

Ch. I A Common Thread
Revelations 19:11–19, Ephesians 6:10–17, 1 Corinthians 12:28

Ch. II The Extremist Within
Revelations 3:15–16, Hebrews 11, Hebrews 11:37–38, Acts 5:32, John 14:15, Acts 19:15, Matthew 25:21, Acts 17:6

Ch. III The Only Easy Day Was Yesterday
Acts 20 and 21, Matthew 24:24, Matthew 24:12–13, Isaiah 17:10–11, Numbers 30:2, Matthew 16:18, Matthew 10:33, Revelation 6:11, 2 Chronicles 16:9, Philippians 3:14,

Ch. IV Jack of All Trades and Masters of None
Romans 8:38–39, Mark 9:23

Ch. V Just Do It!

Matthew 24:15–22, Acts 14:27, John 14:12–13, Acts 5:14–16, John 10:10

Ch. VI The Quiet Professional

John 15:19–21, Luke 17:48, Matthew 11:29, Numbers 12:3

Ch. VII Yes Sir!

Romans 13:1, Hebrews 10:26–31, 1 John 2:4, 1 Corinthians 11:1, Philippians 3:12, 1 Corinthians 15:9, 1 Peter 4:11

Ch. VIII There is no "I" in Team

Matthew 22:39, Romans 8:16–18, John 17:22, 1 Corinthians 2:11, Hebrews 4:12, John 1:1, Romans 8:26–27, Revelations 14:2, 1 Corinthians 12:10, 1 Corinthians 14:5, Ecclesiastes 4:12, Matthew 6:2–4

Ch. IX The Perfect Soldier

1 Corinthians 9:24, Philippians 3:14, Romans 8:29, Matthew 5:48, Deuteronomy 32:4, Romans 6:1, I John 2:4–6, 1 Peter 2:11–13, Jude 1:17–24

Tate Publishing & *Enterprises*

Tate Publishing is commited to excellence in the publishing industry. Our staff of highly trained professionals, including editors, graphic designers, and marketing personnel, work together to produce the very finest books available. The company reflects the philosophy established by the founders, based on Psalms 68:11,

"THE LORD GAVE THE WORD AND GREAT WAS THE COMPANY OF THOSE WHO PUBLISHED IT."

If you would like further information, please call
1.888.361.9473
or visit our website
www.tatepublishing.com

Tate Publishing & *Enterprises*, LLC
127 E. Trade Center Terrace
Mustang, Oklahoma 73064 USA